EASY
Entertaining

Publications International, Ltd.

Favorite Brand Name Recipes at www.fbnr.com

Front cover photography by Proffitt Photography Ltd., Chicago.

Pictured on the front cover: Indian-Spiced Chicken with Wild Rice *(page 110)*.
Pictured on the back cover *(clockwise from top)*: BBQ Pork Sandwiches *(page 150)*, Roasted Mixed Vegetables *(page 216)* and "Red, White and Blue" Mold *(page 282)*.
Pictured on the contents page *(top to bottom)*: Chocolate Waffles *(page 32)* and Philadelphia® 3-Step® Crème Brûlée Cheesecake *(page 342)*.

ISBN: 0-7853-6315-7

Library of Congress Catalog Card Number: 99-067858

Manufactured in China.

8 7 6 5 4 3 2 1

Microwave Cooking: Microwave ovens vary in wattage. Use the cooking times as guidelines and check for doneness before adding more time.

Preparation/Cooking Times: Preparation times are based on the approximate amount of time required to assemble the recipe before cooking, baking, chilling or serving. These times include preparation steps such as measuring, chopping and mixing. The fact that some preparations and cooking can be done simultaneously is taken into account. Preparation of optional ingredients and serving suggestions is not included.

contents

party starters

menu ideas

SUPERBOWL MANIA
Stromboli (page16)

Hot Artichoke Dip (page12)

Nutty Bacon Cheese Ball (page18)

Spicy Mustard Kielbasa Bites (page10)

Guacamole Goal Post Dip (page 266)

menu ideas

A FANCY AFFAIR
Mini Crab Cakes (page 22)

Apple, Goat Cheese & Prosciutto
Bruschetta (page 6)

Savory Stuffed Mushrooms (page 16)

Seafood Spread (page 10)

Peppery Brie en Croûte (page 14)

menu ideas

A TASTE OF THE TROPICS
Frozen Virgin Daiquiris (page 29)

Cilantro-Lime Chicken and
Mango Kabobs (page 23)

Tangy Fruit Kabobs (page12)

*Mini Crab Cakes with Zesty Remoulade
Sauce (page 22)*

Apple, Goat Cheese & Prosciutto Bruschetta

¼ **cup goat cheese, softened at room temperature**

¾ **teaspoon minced fresh thyme leaves,** *or* ¼ **teaspoon dried**

¼ **teaspoon freshly ground black pepper**

8 **slices (or half slices) firm, crusty bread, about 3×4 inches each**

8 **thin slices prosciutto, about ¼ pound**

1 **Fuji apple, cored and very thinly sliced**

1. Preheat broiler. Combine cheese, thyme and black pepper in small bowl; set aside. Place bread on baking sheet; broil, about 6-inches from heat, until lightly toasted. Place prosciutto onto bread. Cut each piece of bread in half and arrange apple slices, then cheese mixture, over prosciutto.

2. Place bruschetta on baking sheet. Broil until cheese softens slightly. Serve as a first course or pass as an hors d'oeuvre.

Makes 16 pieces (4 to 8 servings)

Favorite recipe from Washington Apple Commission

Philly® Pesto Spread

1 **package (8 ounces) PHILADELPHIA® Cream Cheese, softened**

⅓ **cup DI GIORNO® Pesto Sauce**

⅓ **cup chopped tomatoes**

SPREAD cream cheese on serving plate.

TOP with pesto sauce; sprinkle with tomatoes. Serve with crackers.

Makes 10 servings

Prep Time: 5 minutes

Apple, Goat Cheese & Prosciutto Bruschetta

party starters • party starters • party starters • party starters • party starters

party starters • party starters • party starters • party starters • party starters

party starters • party starters • party starters • party starters • party starters

7

Pecan Cheese Ball

1 package (8 ounces) cream cheese, softened

¼ cup finely chopped fresh parsley

2 tablespoons finely chopped fresh chives

½ teaspoon Worcestershire sauce

Dash hot pepper sauce

¾ cup finely chopped pecans

Assorted crackers

Combine all ingredients except pecans and crackers in medium bowl. Cover; refrigerate until firm. Form cheese mixture into a ball. Roll in pecans. Store tightly wrapped in plastic wrap in refrigerator. Allow cheese ball to soften at room temperature before serving with crackers.

Makes 1 cheese ball

Variation: Form cheese mixture into 1½-inch balls. Roll in paprika, chopped herbs, such as parsley, watercress or basil, or chopped green olives instead of pecans.

Gift Tip: Give Pecan Cheese Ball with an assortment of crackers, a wooden cheese board, a jar of imported mustard and/or a bag of pecans.

Garlic Pepper Cheese

8 ounces mozzarella cheese, cut into 6 wedges

2 tablespoons olive oil

1 teaspoon LAWRY'S® Garlic Pepper

In large resealable plastic food storage bag, combine all ingredients; seal bag. Marinate in refrigerator at least 8 hours or overnight. Remove cheese; discard used marinade.

Makes 6 servings

Serving Suggestion: Serve with crackers or sliced French bread, tomato slices and fresh herbs as an appetizer or as a side dish for sandwiches and vegetable platters.

Pecan Cheese Balls

9

Seafood Spread

**1 package (8 ounces)
cream cheese,
softened**

**½ pound smoked
whitefish, skinned,
boned, flaked**

**2 tablespoons minced
green onion**

**1 tablespoon plus
1 teaspoon
chopped fresh dill**

1 teaspoon lemon juice

¼ teaspoon black pepper

Beat cream cheese in medium bowl with electric mixer on medium speed until smooth. Add remaining ingredients, mixing until blended. Refrigerate until ready to serve.

Serve with rye bread slices or assorted crackers. Garnish with lime wedges. *Makes 1½ cups (12 servings)*

Prep Time: 10 minutes plus refrigerating

Spicy Mustard Kielbasa Bites

**1 pound whole kielbasa
or smoked Polish
sausage**

**1 cup FRENCH'S® Deli
Brown Mustard**

¾ cup honey

**1 tablespoon FRANK'S®
REDHOT® Hot Sauce**

1. Place kielbasa on grid. Grill over medium heat 10 minutes or until lightly browned, turning occasionally. Cut into bite-sized pieces; set aside.

2. Combine mustard and honey in large saucepan. Bring to a boil over medium heat. Stir in kielbasa and REDHOT® sauce. Cook until heated through. Transfer to serving bowl. Serve with party toothpicks. *Makes 8 servings*

Seafood Spread

Hot Artichoke Dip

1 can (14 ounces) artichoke hearts, drained, chopped

1 cup (4 ounces) KRAFT® 100% Grated Parmesan Cheese

1 cup KRAFT® Real Mayonnaise or MIRACLE WHIP® Salad Dressing

Chopped tomato

Sliced green onions

MIX all ingredients except tomato and onions in large bowl.

SPOON into 9-inch pie plate or quiche dish.

BAKE at 350°F for 20 to 25 minutes or until lightly browned. Sprinkle with tomato and onions, if desired. Serve with crackers, pita bread triangles or assorted cut-up vegetables.

Makes 8 servings

Spicy Artichoke Dip: Prepare as directed, adding 1 can (4 ounces) chopped green chilies, drained and 1 clove garlic, minced.

Spinach Artichoke Dip: Prepare as directed, adding 1 package (10 ounces) frozen chopped spinach, thawed, drained.

Prep Time: 10 minutes

Bake Time: 25 minutes

Tangy Fruit Kabobs

½ cup drained canned apricot halves

½ cup apple chunks

½ cup banana chunks

¼ cup water

2 tablespoons KIKKOMAN® Soy Sauce

2 tablespoons lemon juice

4 teaspoons sugar

⅛ teaspoon ground cinnamon

Thread apricots, apples and bananas alternately onto 3 (6-inch) metal or bamboo* skewers. Combine water, soy sauce, lemon juice, sugar and cinnamon; brush onto kabobs. Place on grill 4 inches from hot coals; cook 5 minutes or until apples are tender, turning kabobs over and brushing frequently with remaining sauce. (Or, place kabobs on rack of broiler pan. Broil 4 to 5 inches from heat 5 minutes or until apples are tender, turning kabobs over and brushing frequently with remaining sauce.) *Makes 3 servings*

Soak bamboo skewers in water 30 minutes to prevent burning.

Dried Tomato Party Pockets

¼ cup SONOMA® Dried Tomato Bits*

2 tablespoons boiling water

1 cup (4 ounces) shredded sharp Cheddar cheese

3 tablespoons sliced green onions

1 package (10 ounces) prepared refrigerated biscuits (10 biscuits)

1 egg, beaten

2 teaspoons sesame seeds (optional)

*To substitute dried tomato halves for tomato bits, measure ½ cup SONOMA Dried Tomato halves into blender; pulse using on/off button until finely chopped.

Preheat oven to 400°F. Mix tomato bits and water in medium bowl; set aside 5 minutes. Add cheese and onions; toss to blend evenly. Roll out each biscuit to 4- to 5-inch circle on lightly floured surface. For each pocket, place about 2 tablespoons tomato mixture onto center of circle. Brush edge with egg. Fold over and press to seal completely. Place, 2 inches apart, on baking sheet. Brush with egg and sprinkle with sesame seeds, if desired. Bake 10 to 12 minutes or until golden brown. Serve warm or at room temperature. *Makes 10 (4-inch) pockets*

a helping hand

GIVE THIS FLAVORFUL FINGER FOOD SOME CLASS. CREATE A DECORATIVE EDGE BY USING THE TINES OF A FORK TO PRESS THE EDGES TOGETHER.

Peppery Brie en Croûte

2 (4-ounce) packages crescent roll dough

1 (8-ounce) wheel Brie cheese

2 tablespoons TABASCO® brand Green Pepper Sauce

1 egg, beaten

Crackers

Preheat oven to 375°F. Work crescent roll dough into thin circle large enough to completely wrap cheese. Place cheese in center of dough circle. Prick top of cheese several times with fork. Slowly pour 1 tablespoon TABASCO® Green Pepper Sauce over top of cheese. Let stand briefly for sauce to sink in.

Add remaining 1 tablespoon TABASCO® Green Pepper Sauce, pricking cheese several more times with fork. (Some sauce will run over side of cheese.) Bring edges of dough over top of cheese, working it together to completely cover cheese. Brush edges with beaten egg and seal. Bake about 10 minutes, following directions on crescent roll package. (Do not overbake, as cheese will run.) Serve immediately with crackers. *Makes 8 to 10 servings*

Pimiento Cheese Toast

1 loaf French bread, unsliced

1 cup (4 ounces) shredded reduced-fat sharp Cheddar cheese

2 tablespoons diced pimiento

2 tablespoons reduced-fat mayonnaise

1 teaspoon lemon juice

¼ teaspoon dried oregano

1. Slice bread into 8 slices, 1 inch thick each. Toast lightly in toaster or toaster-oven.

2. Combine cheese and pimiento in medium bowl. Stir mayonnaise, lemon juice and oregano together in small bowl; add to cheese mixture. Spread 1 tablespoon mixture onto each slice of toast.

3. Preheat broiler. Place prepared bread on broiler rack. Broil, 4 inches from heat, 2 minutes. Serve immediately.

Makes 8 servings

Peppery Brie en Croûte

Savory Stuffed Mushrooms

20 medium mushrooms

2 tablespoons finely chopped onion

2 tablespoons finely chopped red bell pepper

3 tablespoons FLEISCHMANN'S® Original Margarine

½ cup dry seasoned bread crumbs

½ teaspoon dried basil leaves

1. Remove stems from mushrooms; finely chop ¼ cup stems.

2. Cook and stir chopped stems, onion and pepper in margarine in skillet over medium heat until tender. Remove from heat; stir in crumbs and basil.

3. Spoon crumb mixture loosely into mushroom caps; place on baking sheet. Bake at 400°F for 15 minutes or until hot.

Makes 20 appetizers

Prep Time: 20 minutes

Cook Time: 15 minutes

Total Time: 35 minutes

Stromboli

1 package (10 ounces) refrigerated pizza dough

⅓ cup FRENCH'S® Deli Mustard

¾ pound sliced deli meats and cheese such as salami, provolone cheese and ham

1 egg, beaten

1 teaspoon poppy or sesame seeds

1. Preheat oven to 425°F. Unroll pizza dough on lightly floured board. Roll into 13×10-inch rectangle. Spread mustard evenly on dough. Layer luncheon meats on dough, overlapping slices, leaving a 1-inch border around edges.

2. Fold one-third of dough toward center from long edge. Fold second side toward center enclosing filling. Pinch long edge to seal. Pinch ends together, tuck under dough. Place on greased baking sheet. Cut shallow crosswise slits on top of dough, spacing 3-inches apart. Brush with beaten egg; sprinkle with poppy seeds. Bake 15 to 18 minutes or until deep golden brown. Remove to rack; cool slightly. Serve warm.

Makes 12 servings

Savory Stuffed Mushrooms

Nutty Bacon Cheeseball

1 package (8 ounces) cream cheese, softened

½ cup milk

2 cups (8 ounces) shredded sharp Cheddar cheese

2 cups (8 ounces) shredded Monterey Jack cheese

¼ cup (1 ounce) crumbled blue cheese

¼ cup finely minced green onions (white parts only)

1 jar (2 ounces) diced pimento, undrained

10 slices bacon, cooked, drained, finely crumbled and divided

¾ cup finely chopped pecans, divided

Salt and pepper to taste

¼ cup minced parsley

1 tablespoon poppy seeds

Beat cream cheese and milk with electric mixer on low speed in large bowl until blended. Add cheeses. Blend on medium speed until well combined. Add green onions, pimento, half of bacon and half of pecans. Blend on medium speed until well mixed. Add salt and pepper to taste. Transfer half of mixture to large piece of plastic wrap. Form into ball; wrap tightly. Repeat with remaining mixture. Refrigerate until chilled, at least two hours.

Combine remaining bacon and pecans with parsley and poppy seeds in pie plate or large dinner plate. Remove plastic wrap from each ball; roll each in bacon mixture until well coated. Wrap each ball tightly in plastic wrap and refrigerate until ready to use, up to 24 hours. *Makes about 24 servings*

personal touch

DEVOTE MORE TIME TO YOUR GUESTS AND SPEND LESS TIME IN THE KITCHEN BY MAKING THIS APPETIZER THE DAY BEFORE. SIMPLY TAKE THE CHEESE BALL OUT OF THE REFRIGERATOR THE DAY OF THE PARTY, ARRANGE CRACKERS AND VEGETABLES FOR DIPPERS AND YOU'RE READY TO RELAX WITH YOUR GUESTS.

Nutty Bacon Cheeseball

Three Mushroom Ratatouille

1 package (3½ ounces) fresh shiitake mushrooms*

1 tablespoon olive oil

1 large onion, chopped

4 cloves garlic, minced

1 package (8 ounces) button mushrooms, chopped

1 package (6 ounces) crimini mushrooms, chopped

1 cup chicken broth

½ cup chopped fresh tomato

2 tablespoons chopped fresh parsley

2 tablespoons grated Parmesan cheese

3 pita breads (6 inches each)

Italian parsley for garnish

*Or, substitute 1 ounce dried black Chinese mushrooms. Place dried mushrooms in small bowl; cover with warm water. Soak 20 minutes to soften. Drain; squeeze out excess moisture. Prepare as directed in Step 1.

1. Remove stems from shiitake mushrooms; discard stems and chop caps.

2. Preheat broiler. Heat oil in large skillet over medium heat until hot. Add onion and garlic. Cook 5 minutes, stirring occasionally. Add mushrooms; cook 5 minutes more, stirring often.

3. Add chicken broth; bring to a boil. Cook about 10 minutes or until liquid is absorbed. Remove from heat. Stir in tomato, chopped parsley and cheese. Spoon into bowl.

4. Meanwhile, split each pita bread horizontally in half. Stack halves; cut stack into 6 wedges. Arrange wedges in single layer on baking sheet. Broil 4 inches from heat 1 to 3 minutes or until wedges are toasted.

5. Arrange toasted pita bread triangles and warm dip in basket. Garnish, if desired.   *Makes about 2¼ cups*

Three Mushroom Ratatouille

Mini Crab Cakes

1 pound crabmeat

1 cup fine, dry bread crumbs, divided

2 eggs, beaten

¼ cup minced onion

¼ cup minced green bell pepper

¼ cup minced red bell pepper

1 teaspoon dry mustard

½ teaspoon TABASCO® brand Pepper Sauce

Salt to taste

Vegetable oil

Zesty Remoulade Sauce (recipe follows)

Fresh dill (optional)

Combine crabmeat, ½ cup bread crumbs, eggs, onion, bell peppers, mustard, TABASCO® Sauce and salt in large bowl. Cover and refrigerate 1 to 2 hours or until mixture becomes firm. Shape mixture into small cakes, about 1×1½ inches. Coat cakes in remaining ½ cup bread crumbs.

Pour oil into heavy skillet to depth of ⅓ inch; heat skillet over medium heat. When oil is hot, cook crab cakes about 3 to 5 minutes on each side or until browned. Remove to paper towels. Serve crab cakes warm; top with dollops of Zesty Remoulade Sauce. Garnish with dill sprigs, if desired.   *Makes 20 to 25 cakes*

Zesty Remoulade Sauce

1 cup mayonnaise

2 to 3 green onions, finely chopped

1 celery stalk, finely chopped

2 tablespoons prepared horseradish, drained

1 tablespoon finely chopped chives

1 tablespoon Dijon mustard

1 tablespoon fresh lemon juice

1 clove garlic, finely chopped

½ teaspoon TABASCO® brand Pepper Sauce

Combine all ingredients in medium bowl. Cover and refrigerate 1 hour to blend flavors. Serve chilled.

Cilantro-Lime Chicken and Mango Kabobs

1 pound boneless skinless chicken breasts, cut into thin strips

1 large mango, peeled and cut into chunks

1 large green pepper, cut into 1-inch squares

3 tablespoons honey

3 tablespoons lime juice

1 teaspoon grated lime peel

2 tablespoons FLEISCHMANN'S® Original Margarine

2 tablespoons chopped cilantro or parsley

Thread chicken, mango and pepper alternately on 8 skewers; set aside.

In small saucepan, over medium heat, heat honey, lime juice, lime peel, margarine and cilantro until hot. Keep warm.

Broil or grill kabobs 4 inches from heat 12 to 15 minutes or until chicken is cooked, turning and brushing with honey mixture often. Reheat any remaining honey mixture to a boil; serve with kabobs.

Makes 8 appetizers or 4 main-dish servings

Guacamole

2 large avocados

2 teaspoons lemon juice

¼ teaspoon LAWRY'S® Seasoned Salt

In small bowl, coarsely mash avocados; add lemon juice and Seasoned Salt. Mix well.   *Makes about 1½ cups*

Serving Suggestion: Serve immediately or cover tightly and refrigerate until serving time.

Pepperidge Farm® Savory Criss-Cross Pastry

½ **package (17¼-ounce size) PEPPERIDGE FARM® Frozen Puff Pastry Sheets (1 sheet)**

2 eggs

1 tablespoon water

½ **pound bulk pork sausage**

1 cup PEPPERIDGE FARM® Herb Seasoned Stuffing

1 small onion, chopped (about ¼ cup)

1 cup chopped mushrooms (about 3 ounces)

1. Thaw pastry sheet at room temperature 30 minutes. Preheat oven to 375°F. Mix 1 egg and water and set aside.

2. Mix sausage, stuffing, remaining egg, onion and mushrooms **thoroughly.**

3. Unfold pastry on lightly floured surface. Cut slits 1 inch apart from outer edge up to fold mark on each side of pastry. Spoon sausage mixture down center of pastry. Starting at one end, fold pastry strips over stuffing mixture, alternating sides, to cover sausage mixture. Place on baking sheet. Brush with egg mixture.

4. Bake 35 minutes or until golden. Slice and serve warm.

Makes 4 main-dish servings or 8 appetizer servings

Thaw Time: 30 minutes

Prep Time: 20 minutes

Cook Time: 35 minutes

personal touch

MIX IT UP! TO GET THE PARTY STARTED PLAY A VARIETY OF BACKGROUND MUSIC EVERYONE WILL ENJOY. CHOOSE SELECTIONS FROM R&B TO CLASSICAL TO JAZZ.

Pepperidge Farm® Savory Criss-Cross Pastry

Classic Bloody Mary

1 quart tomato juice

1 cup vodka

1 tablespoon Worcestershire sauce

1 tablespoon fresh lime juice

½ teaspoon TABASCO® brand Pepper Sauce

Lime slices for garnish (optional)

Celery ribs for garnish (optional)

Combine all ingredients except garnishes in 2-quart pitcher. Stir well. Serve over ice. Garnish with lime slices or celery, if desired.

Makes 6 (6-ounce) servings

Bronze Nectarine Margaritas

10 Frozen California Nectarine Cubes (recipe follows)

¾ cup orange juice

2 tablespoons lime juice

2 tablespoons sugar

10 ice cubes, cracked

Combine all ingredients in blender or food processor; process until smooth. Pour into stemmed glasses. *Makes 2 servings*

Frozen California Nectarine Cubes: Slice 4 fresh nectarines. Combine in blender or food processor with ¼ cup lime juice; process. Pour into ice cube trays; freeze. Makes 20 cubes.

Favorite recipe from California Tree Fruit Agreement

Classic Bloody Mary

Cranberry-Orange Cooler

1 cup boiling water

1 package (4-serving size) JELL-O® Brand Orange Flavor Gelatin

2½ cups cranberry juice, chilled

Ice cubes (optional)

Orange slices (optional)

STIR boiling water into gelatin in large bowl at least 2 minutes until completely dissolved. Add cranberry juice. Pour over ice cubes in tall glasses and garnish with orange slices, if desired.

Makes about 3½ cups

Prep Time: 5 minutes

Peach Fizz

3 fresh California peaches, peeled, halved, pitted and sliced

1 can (6 ounces) pineapple juice

¼ cup frozen limeade or lemonade concentrate

¼ teaspoon almond extract

Finely crushed ice

3 cups club soda, chilled

Add peaches to food processor or blender. Process until smooth to measure 2 cups purée. Stir in pineapple juice, limeade and almond extract. Fill 12-ounce glasses ⅔ full with crushed ice. Add ⅓ cup peach base to each. Top with club soda. Stir gently. Serve immediately.

Makes 6 servings

Favorite recipe from California Tree Fruit Agreement

Frozen Virgin Daiquiris

1 can (12 ounces) frozen DOLE® Pineapple Juice Concentrate, divided

3 cups water, divided

1 teaspoon rum extract (optional), divided

4 cups ice cubes, divided

- Place half of frozen juice concentrate, water, rum extract and ice cubes in blender or food processor container. Blend until mixture is slushy.
- Pour into tall glasses or large pitcher; set aside.
- Repeat blending with remaining ingredients.
- Stir before serving. Serve immediately.   *Makes 10 servings*

Prep Time: 10 minutes

Mango Smoothie

½ cup low-fat plain yogurt

1 ripe mango, peeled, seeded and sliced

¼ cup orange-pineapple juice

1 teaspoon honey

2 ice cubes

Fresh mint leaves for garnish

Place all ingredients except mint leaves in blender container. Cover; blend until smooth. (Add milk if thinner consistency is desired.) Garnish, if desired.   *Makes 1 serving*

a helping hand

VARYING IN SIZE, SHAPE AND COLOR, THE YELLOWISH ORANGE FLESH OF THE MANGO HAS A RICH FLAVOR AND A SPICY AROMA. MANGOS MUST BE FULLY RIPE BEFORE EATING OR USING IN RECIPES. ALLOW THEM TO RIPEN AT ROOM TEMPERATURE UNTIL SOFT, THEN USE OR REFRIGERATE FOR A FEW DAYS.

morning glories

menu ideas

LUMBERJACK BUFFET

Egg and Sausage Breakfast Strudel
(page 50)

Buttermilk Pancakes with
Blueberry-Orange Sauce (page 78)

Sweet and Russet Potato Latkes
(page 42)

Bacon Cheese Muffins (page 67)

menu ideas

THE BREAD BASKET

Cherry Cheese Danish Ring (page 66)

Mini-Sticky Pecan Buns (page 55)

Blueberry Orange Muffins (page 72)

Brunch-Time Zucchini-Date Break
(page 34)

Cranberry Scones (page 76)

menu ideas

CHRISTMAS MORNING
BREAKFAST

Make-Ahead Breakfast Casserole
(page 44)

Hot Cross Buns (page 70)

Cinnamon Sugared
Pumpkin-Pecan Muffins (page 48)

Cherry Cheese Danish Ring (page 66)

Chocolate Waffles

2 cups all-purpose flour

¼ cup unsweetened cocoa powder

2 tablespoons sugar

1 tablespoon baking powder

½ teaspoon salt

2 cups milk

2 eggs, beaten

¼ cup vegetable oil

1 teaspoon vanilla extract

Raspberry Syrup (recipe follows)

1. Preheat waffle iron; grease lightly.

2. Sift flour, cocoa, sugar, baking powder and salt into large bowl. Combine milk, eggs, oil and vanilla in small bowl. Stir liquid ingredients into dry ingredients until moistened.

3. For each waffle, pour about ¾ cup batter into waffle iron. Close lid and bake until steaming stops.* Serve with Raspberry Syrup.

Makes about 6 waffles

Check manufacturer's directions for recommended amount of batter and baking time.

Raspberry Syrup

1 cup water

1 cup sugar

1 package (10 ounces) frozen raspberries in syrup

Combine water and sugar in large saucepan. Cook over medium heat, stirring constantly, until sugar has dissolved. Continue cooking until mixture thickens slightly, about 10 minutes.

Stir in frozen raspberries; cook, stirring, until berries are thawed. Bring to a boil; continue stirring until syrup thickens slightly, about 10 minutes. Serve warm.

Chocolate Waffles

Brunch-Time Zucchini-Date Bread

1 cup chopped, pitted dates

1 cup water

1 cup whole wheat flour

1 cup all-purpose flour

2 tablespoons sugar

1 teaspoon baking powder

½ teaspoon baking soda

½ teaspoon salt

½ teaspoon ground cinnamon

¼ teaspoon ground cloves

2 eggs

1 cup shredded zucchini, pressed dry with paper towels

1 package (8 ounces) fat-free cream cheese

¼ cup powdered sugar

1 tablespoon vanilla

⅛ teaspoon ground cinnamon

Dash ground cloves

1. Preheat oven to 350°F. Spray 8×4×2-inch loaf pan with nonstick cooking spray.

2. Combine dates and water in small saucepan. Bring to a boil over medium-high heat. Remove from heat; let stand 15 minutes.

3. Combine flours, sugar, baking powder, baking soda, salt, cinnamon and cloves in large bowl. Beat eggs in medium bowl; stir in date mixture and zucchini. Stir egg mixture into flour mixture just until dry ingredients are moistened. Pour batter evenly into prepared pan.

4. Bake 30 to 35 minutes or until toothpick inserted into center comes out clean. Cool 5 minutes. Remove from pan. Cool completely on wire rack.

5. Meanwhile, to prepare cheese spread, combine fat-free cream cheese, sugar, vanilla, cinnamon and cloves in small bowl. Beat until smooth. Cover and refrigerate until ready to use.

6. Cut bread into 16 slices. Serve with cheese spread.

Makes 16 servings

personal touch

STOP THE PASSING! TO AVOID THE CONSTANT MOVEMENT OF THE CHEESE SPREAD, DIVIDE IT BETWEEN TWO OR THREE CONTAINERS THAT CAN BE PLACED AT DIFFERENT PARTS OF THE TABLE. THIS WILL ALLOW GUEST TO ENGAGE IN MORE ENJOYABLE CONVERSATION THAN "PLEASE PASS THE CHEESE SPREAD."

Brunch-Time Zucchini-Date Bread

Strawberry & Banana Stuffed French Toast

1 loaf (12 inches) French bread

2 tablespoons strawberry jam

4 ounces cream cheese, softened

¼ cup chopped strawberries

¼ cup chopped banana

6 eggs, lightly beaten

¾ cup milk

3 tablespoons butter or margarine, divided

Strawberry Sauce (recipe follows)

1. Cut French bread into eight 1½-inch slices. Make pocket in each slice by cutting through top crust and almost to bottom, leaving sides of bread slices intact.

2. Combine jam, cream cheese, strawberries and banana in small bowl to make filling.

3. Place heaping tablespoon of strawberry filling into each pocket. Press back together.

4. Beat eggs and milk in wide shallow bowl. Add bread; let stand to coat, then turn to coat other side.

5. Heat 2 tablespoons butter in large skillet over medium-low heat. Add as many bread slices as will fit; cook until brown. Turn and cook other side. Remove and keep warm. Repeat with remaining butter and bread slices. Serve with Strawberry Sauce.

Makes 8 slices

Strawberry Sauce: Combine 1 pint hulled strawberries, 2 to 3 tablespoons sugar and 1 tablespoon strawberry- or orange-flavored liqueur in blender or food processor. Cover; process until strawberries are puréed. Makes 1½ cups.

Strawberry & Banana Stuffed French Toast

Encore Eggs Benedict

**Hollandaise Sauce
(recipe follows)**

8 eggs

16 slices Canadian bacon

**4 English muffins, split,
toasted and
buttered**

a helping hand

LEGEND HAS IT THAT
EGGS BENEDICT
ORIGINATED AT THE
FAMOUS
DELMONICO'S
RESTAURANT IN
MANHATTAN WHERE
ONE DAY THE
MAITRE D' AND
MRS. BENEDICT
BEGAN DISCUSSING
NEW OPTIONS FOR
THE LUNCH MENU.
FROM THIS
DISCUSSION, EGGS
BENEDICT WAS
CREATED.

1. Prepare Hollandaise Sauce.

2. Bring 2 to 3 inches water to a boil in medium saucepan over medium-high heat. Reduce heat to a simmer. Break 1 egg into small dish. Holding dish close to surface of simmering water, carefully slip egg into water. Repeat with 1 egg. Cook 3 to 5 minutes or until yolks are just set. Remove eggs and drain on paper towels. Repeat with remaining eggs.

3. Cook bacon in large skillet over medium-low heat, turning occasionally.

4. Top each English muffin half with 2 slices bacon, 1 poached egg and 1 tablespoon Hollandaise Sauce. Serve immediately.

Makes 4 servings

Hollandaise Sauce

3 egg yolks

1 tablespoon lemon juice

1 teaspoon dry mustard

¼ teaspoon salt

Dash ground red pepper (optional)

½ cup (1 stick) butter, cut into eighths

1. Beat together egg yolks, lemon juice, mustard, salt and pepper in small saucepan until blended. Add ½ of butter.

2. Cook over low heat, stirring with wire whisk until butter is melted. Slowly add remaining ¼ cup butter; whisk constantly until butter is melted and sauce is thickened. *Makes ¾ cup*

Encore Eggs Benedict

Banana-Walnut Bread

5 tablespoons margarine, softened

½ cup granulated sugar

½ cup packed light brown sugar

1 whole egg

2 egg whites

1 teaspoon vanilla

1 ½ cups mashed, very ripe bananas

1 ¾ cups all-purpose flour

1 teaspoon baking soda

¼ teaspoon baking powder

½ teaspoon salt

½ cup apple or orange juice

⅓ cup (2 ounces) coarsely chopped black or English walnuts

1. Preheat oven to 350°F. Spray bottom only of 9×5×3-inch loaf pan with nonstick cooking spray.

2. Beat margarine in large bowl with electric mixer until fluffy. Beat in granulated and brown sugars. Beat in whole egg, egg whites and vanilla. Mix in bananas, beating at high speed 30 seconds.

3. Combine flour, baking soda, baking powder and salt in medium bowl. Add to margarine mixture alternately with apple juice, ending with flour mixture. Stir in walnuts.

4. Pour batter evenly into prepared loaf pan. Bake about 1 hour 15 minutes or until browned and toothpick inserted near center comes out clean.

5. Cool bread in pan on wire rack 10 minutes. Remove bread from pan; cool completely on wire rack. Garnish as desired.

Makes 1 loaf (about 18 slices)

personal touch

BANANAS OVERRIPE? DON'T THROW THEM OUT. SIMPLY PLACE THEM IN AN AIRTIGHT RESEALABLE FREEZER BAG AND FREEZE UP TO 6 MONTHS. WHEN YOU ARE READY TO USE THEM, BRING THEM TO ROOM TEMPERATURE AND MASH FOR BANANA BREAD.

Creamy Fruit Blintzes

CHEESE FILLING

1 egg yolk

2 tablespoons sugar

1 (8-ounce) package cream cheese, softened

2 cups (12-ounce carton) dry or creamed cottage cheese

¼ teaspoon vanilla

BLINTZES

3 eggs

3 tablespoons oil

1½ cups milk

1 cup all-purpose flour

½ teaspoon salt

⅓ cup butter or margarine, melted

2 tablespoons butter or margarine (unmelted)

Powdered sugar

1 cup sour cream

1 cup (12-ounce jar) SMUCKER'S® Strawberry, Cherry or Blueberry Preserves

Combine egg yolk and sugar; beat with electric mixer until thick and yellow. Add cream cheese, cottage cheese and vanilla; mix well. Refrigerate until ready to use.

Combine eggs, oil and milk; beat with electric mixer until well blended. Add flour and salt; continue to beat until batter is smooth and flour is dissolved. Refrigerate, covered, for 30 minutes or until ready to use.

Slowly heat small skillet. To test temperature, drop a little cold water onto surface; water should bead up and bounce. For each blintz, brush pan lightly with melted butter. Measure 3 tablespoons of batter into cup. Pour in all at once, rotating skillet quickly to spread evenly. Cook for 1 minute until golden brown on underside; loosen edge with spatula and remove. Dry on paper towels. Stack, brown side up, with waxed paper between blitzes.

Spread 3 tablespoons of filling on browned side of each blintz, making a rectangle 4 inches long. Fold two sides in over filling, overlapping edges and covering filling completely. Melt 1 tablespoon butter in large skillet over medium heat. Place half of blintzes, seam-side-down and not touching in skillet. Cook until golden brown, turning once. Keep warm in low oven while cooking second half of blintzes. Serve hot, sprinkled with powdered sugar and topped with sour cream and preserves.

Makes 16 blintzes (8 servings)

Note: All four sides of blintzes may be folded in, overlapping edges to form a square. Filling is completely enclosed.

Sweet and Russet Potato Latkes

2 cups shredded russet potatoes

1 cup shredded sweet potato

1 cup shredded apple

¾ cup cholesterol-free egg substitute

⅓ cup all-purpose flour

1 teaspoon sugar

¼ teaspoon baking powder

¼ teaspoon salt

⅛ teaspoon ground nutmeg

Nonstick cooking spray

1 cup unsweetened cinnamon applesauce

1. Combine potatoes and apple in medium bowl. Combine egg substitute, flour, sugar, baking powder, salt and nutmeg in small bowl; add to potato mixture.

2. Spray large nonstick skillet with cooking spray; heat over medium-low heat until hot. Spoon 1 rounded tablespoonful of potato mixture into skillet to form pancake about ¼ inch thick and 3 inches in diameter.* Cook 3 minutes or until browned. Turn latke and cook second side 3 minutes or until browned. Repeat with remaining batter. Keep cooked latkes warm in preheated 250°F oven.

3. Top each latke with 1 tablespoon applesauce. Garnish, if desired. *Makes 8 (2-latke) servings*

Three to four latkes can be cooked at one time.

personal touch

ADD A SPECIAL TOUCH TO YOUR BREAKFAST BUFFET BY SERVING FLAVORED CREAMERS, BROWNULATED SUGAR, GROUND CINNAMON, GROUND NUTMEG AND SWEETENED COCOA POWDER FOR YOUR GUESTS TO ADD TO THEIR COFFEE.

Sweet and Russet Potato Latkes

Make-Ahead Breakfast Casserole

2½ cups seasoned croutons

1 pound BOB EVANS® Original Recipe Roll Sausage

4 eggs

2¼ cups milk

1 (10½-ounce) can condensed cream of mushroom soup

1 (10-ounce) package frozen chopped spinach, thawed and squeezed dry

1 (4-ounce) can mushrooms, drained and chopped

1 cup (4 ounces) shredded sharp Cheddar cheese

1 cup (4 ounces) shredded Monterey Jack cheese

¼ teaspoon dry mustard

Fresh herb sprigs and carrot strips (optional)

Picante sauce or salsa (optional)

Spread croutons on bottom of greased 13×9-inch baking dish. Crumble sausage into medium skillet. Cook over medium heat until browned, stirring occasionally. Drain off any drippings. Spread over croutons. Whisk eggs and milk in large bowl until blended. Stir in soup, spinach, mushrooms, cheeses and mustard. Pour egg mixture over sausage and croutons. Refrigerate overnight. Preheat oven to 325°F. Bake egg mixture 50 to 55 minutes or until set and lightly browned on top. Garnish with herb sprigs and carrot, if desired. Serve hot with picante sauce, if desired. Refrigerate leftovers. *Makes 10 to 12 servings*

personal touch

CANDLELIGHT ISN'T JUST FOR EVENINGS! START THE DAY OFF RIGHT BY CREATING A RELAXING AND COZY ENVIRONMENT. PLACE CANDLES ON THE TABLE AND THROUGHOUT THE HOUSE.

Make-Ahead Breakfast Casserole

Fruited Granola

3 cups uncooked oats

1 cup sliced unblanched almonds

1 cup honey

3 tablespoons butter or margarine, melted

½ cup wheat germ or honey wheat germ

1 teaspoon ground cinnamon

3 cups whole grain or whole wheat cereal flakes

½ cup dried blueberries or golden raisins

½ cup dried cranberries or tart cherries

½ cup dried banana chips or chopped pitted dates

1. Preheat oven to 325°F. Spread oats and almonds in single layer in 13×9-inch baking pan. Bake 15 minutes or until lightly toasted, stirring frequently with wooden spoon. Remove pan from oven. Set aside.

2. Combine honey, butter, wheat germ and cinnamon in large bowl with wooden spoon until well blended. Add oats and almonds; toss to coat completely. Spread mixture in single layer in baking pan with wooden spoon.

3. Bake 20 minutes or until golden brown. Cool completely in pan on wire rack. Break mixture into chunks with wooden spoon.

4. Combine oat chunks, cereal, blueberries, cranberries and banana chips in large bowl.

5. Store in airtight container at room temperature up to 2 weeks.

Makes about 10 cups

Fruited Granola

Cinnamon Sugared Pumpkin-Pecan Muffins

½ cup granulated sugar, divided

2½ to 3 teaspoons ground cinnamon, divided

1 cup 100% bran cereal

1 cup fat-free (skim) milk

1 cup all-purpose flour

1 tablespoon baking powder

½ teaspoon baking soda

½ teaspoon salt

1 cup canned pumpkin

1 egg, beaten

1 tablespoon vanilla extract

1 package (2 ounces) pecan chips

Preheat oven to 400°F. Coat nonstick 12-cup muffin pan with nonstick cooking spray. Combine 2 tablespoons sugar and ½ to 1 teaspoon cinnamon in small bowl for topping; set aside.

Blend cereal and milk in large bowl; set aside 5 minutes to soften. Meanwhile, combine flour, remaining sugar and cinnamon, baking powder, baking soda and salt in large bowl; mix well.

Whisk pumpkin, egg and vanilla into softened cereal. Gently fold in flour mixture just until blended. *Do not overmix.* Spoon equal amounts of batter into each muffin cup; sprinkle evenly with pecan chips. Sprinkle with reserved cinnamon-sugar topping.

Bake 20 to 25 minutes. Cool on wire rack 3 minutes before removing muffins from pan. Serve warm or at room temperature.

Makes 12 muffins

a helping hand

TO KEEP MUFFINS WARM, LINE A BREAD BASKET WITH FOIL, CUT OFF AT THE RIM, AND THEN A NAPKIN. BE SURE THE NAPKIN IS LARGE ENOUGH TO FOLD OVER THE MUFFINS ONCE PLACED IN THE BASKET. THIS WILL KEEP THEM FROM DRYING OUT AND KEEP THE HEAT IN.

Cinnamon Sugared Pumpkin-Pecan Muffins

Egg and Sausage Breakfast Strudel

1 pound BOB EVANS® Original Recipe Roll Sausage

¾ cup finely grated Parmesan cheese

1 (10¾-ounce) can condensed cream of mushroom soup

2 hard-cooked eggs, cut into ¼-inch cubes

½ cup thinly sliced green onions

¼ cup chopped fresh parsley

1 (16-ounce) package frozen phyllo dough, thawed according to package directions

Butter-flavored nonstick cooking spray *or* ½ cup melted butter or margarine

Crumble and cook sausage in medium skillet until browned. Drain off any drippings; place in medium bowl. Add cheese, soup, eggs, green onions and parsley; stir gently until blended. Cover and chill at least 4 hours.

Preheat oven to 375°F. Layer 4 sheets of phyllo dough, coating each sheet with cooking spray or brushing with melted butter before stacking. Cut stack in half lengthwise. Shape ⅓ cup filling into log and place at bottom end of 1 stack. Fold in sides to cover filling; roll up phyllo dough and filling jelly roll style. Seal edges and spray roll with cooking spray or brush with butter. Repeat with remaining phyllo dough and filling. Place rolls on ungreased baking sheet, seam sides down. Bake 15 to 20 minutes or until golden brown. Serve hot. Refrigerate leftovers. *Makes 10 strudels*

Note: Unbaked strudels can be wrapped and refrigerated up to 24 hours, or frozen up to 1 month. If frozen, allow additional baking time.

Egg and Sausage Breakfast Strudel

Orange Cinnamon Swirl Bread

BREAD
1 package DUNCAN HINES® Cinnamon Swirl Muffin Mix

1 egg

⅔ cup orange juice

1 tablespoon grated orange peel

ORANGE GLAZE
½ cup confectioners' sugar

2 to 3 teaspoons orange juice

1 teaspoon grated orange peel

Quartered orange slices, for garnish (optional)

1. Preheat oven to 350°F. Grease and flour 8½×4½×2½-inch loaf pan.

2. For bread, combine muffin mix and contents of topping packet from mix in large bowl. Break up any lumps. Add egg, ⅔ cup orange juice and 1 tablespoon orange peel. Stir until moistened, about 50 strokes. Knead swirl packet from mix for 10 seconds before opening. Squeeze contents on top of batter. Swirl into batter with knife or spatula, folding from bottom of bowl to get an even swirl. *Do not completely mix in.* Pour into pan. Bake at 350°F 55 to 60 minutes or until toothpick inserted in center comes out clean. Cool in pan 10 minutes. Loosen loaf from pan. Invert onto cooling rack. Turn right side up. Cool completely.

3. For orange glaze, place confectioners' sugar in small bowl. Add orange juice, 1 teaspoon at a time, stirring until smooth and desired consistency. Stir in 1 teaspoon orange peel. Drizzle over loaf. Garnish with orange slices, if desired.

Makes 1 loaf (12 slices)

Tip: If glaze becomes too thin, add more confectioners' sugar. If glaze is too thick, add more orange juice.

Orange Cinnamon Swirl Bread

Cake Doughnuts

3¾ cups all-purpose flour

1 tablespoon baking powder

¾ teaspoon salt

1 teaspoon ground cinnamon

½ teaspoon ground nutmeg

3 eggs

¾ cup granulated sugar

1 cup applesauce

2 tablespoons butter or margarine, melted and cooled slightly

2 cups sifted powdered sugar

3 tablespoons milk

½ teaspoon vanilla

1 quart vegetable oil for frying

1. Combine flour, baking powder, salt, cinnamon and nutmeg in medium bowl; set aside.

2. Beat eggs in large bowl with electric mixer at high speed until frothy. Gradually beat in granulated sugar. Continue beating at high speed 4 minutes until thick and lemon colored, scraping down side of bowl once.

3. Reduce speed to low; beat in applesauce and butter. Beat in flour mixture until well blended, scraping down side of bowl once.

4. Spoon half of dough onto sheet of plastic wrap. Spread dough into 5-inch square; wrap square in another sheet of plastic wrap. Repeat with remaining dough. Refrigerate about 3 hours or until well chilled.

5. To prepare glaze, combine powdered sugar, milk and vanilla in small bowl until smooth. Cover; set aside.

6. Pour oil into 6-quart Dutch oven. Insert deep-fat thermometer. Heat oil over medium heat until thermometer registers 375°F; adjust heat to maintain temperature.

7. Meanwhile, roll out one piece dough to ⅜-inch thickness on well-floured pastry cloth with well-floured rolling pin. Cut dough with floured 3-inch doughnut cutter; repeat with remaining dough. Reroll scraps, reserving doughnut holes.

8. Place 4 doughnuts and holes on large plate. Carefully slide into hot oil, 1 at a time. Cook 2 minutes or until golden brown on both sides, turning often. Remove with slotted spoon; drain on paper-towel-lined plate. Repeat with remaining doughnuts and holes.

9. Spread glaze over warm doughnuts with small metal spatula. (Doughnuts can also be dipped into glaze.) Best when served warm. *Makes 1 dozen doughnuts and holes*

Potato & Onion Frittata

1 small baking potato, peeled, halved and sliced ⅛-inch thick (about ½ cup)

¼ cup chopped onion

1 clove garlic, minced

Dash ground black pepper

1 tablespoon FLEISCHMANN'S® Original Margarine

1 cup EGG BEATERS® Healthy Real Egg Product

In 8-inch nonstick skillet, over medium-high heat, sauté potato, onion, garlic and pepper in margarine until tender. Pour Egg Beaters evenly into skillet over potato mixture. Cook without stirring for 5 to 6 minutes or until cooked on bottom and almost set on top. Carefully turn frittata; cook for 1 to 2 minutes more or until done. Slide onto serving platter; cut into wedges to serve.

Makes 2 servings

Prep Time: 5 minutes

Cook Time: 15 minutes

Mini-Sticky Pecan Buns

1 package BOB EVANS® Frozen White Dinner Roll Dough

½ cup packed brown sugar

2 teaspoons ground cinnamon

½ cup finely chopped pecans

½ cup melted butter

Thaw dough at room temperature 45 minutes to 1 hour; do not allow dough to begin rising. Divide each piece of dough into 4 equal pieces; roll each piece in tight circle to form a ball with smooth surface. Combine sugar, cinnamon and pecans in shallow dish. Dip dough balls in melted butter and roll in sugar mixture. Arrange in 2 layers in well-greased 10-inch tube pan, allowing space for dough to rise. Combine any remaining butter and sugar mixture; pour over rolls. Cover pan with damp towel; allow to rise at room temperature until doubled in bulk. Preheat oven to 350°F. Bake 30 minutes or until light golden in color. Let stand 10 to 15 minutes before turning out of pan onto serving plate. Serve warm.

Makes 8 to 10 servings

Bagels

6 BAGELS

1 cup plus 3 tablespoons
water

2 tablespoons sugar

1 ½ teaspoons salt

3 cups bread flour

2 teaspoons rapid-rise
yeast

9 BAGELS

1 ½ cups water

3 tablespoons sugar

2 teaspoons salt

4 cups bread flour

2 teaspoons rapid-rise
yeast

FOR BOILING AND BAKING:

3 quarts water

1 tablespoon sugar

2 to 3 tablespoons
cornmeal

1 egg, beaten

1 to 2 tablespoons
sesame seeds,
poppy seeds,
caraway seeds or
cinnamon sugar
(optional)

1. Measure carefully, placing all ingredients except those required for boiling and baking in bread machine pan in order specified by owner's manual. Program dough cycle setting; press start.

2. Turn out dough onto floured surface; knead briefly. Cut into 6 pieces for small batch or 9 pieces for large batch. Shape into balls. Place on floured surface; let rest 10 minutes. Poke thumb through center of each ball to make hole. Stretch into doughnut shapes. Place back on floured surface. Let rise, uncovered, 15 minutes or until puffy. *Do not overproof bagels.*

3. For boiling and baking, preheat oven to 400°F. Bring water and sugar to a boil in large, deep skillet or wok. Spray 2 baking sheets with nonstick cooking spray; sprinkle with cornmeal. Carefully lower bagels, 3 at a time, into boiling water. Boil 5 minutes, turning often. Remove bagels using slotted spoon; drain briefly on paper towels. Place 2 inches apart on prepared baking sheets. Brush with beaten egg and sprinkle with sesame seeds, if desired. Bake 25 to 30 minutes or until golden brown. Remove from baking sheets; cool on wire rack. *Makes 6 or 9 bagels*

Bagels

French Toast Strata

4 ounces day-old French or Italian bread, cut into ¾-inch cubes (4 cups)

⅓ cup golden raisins

1 package (3 ounces) cream cheese, cut into ¼-inch cubes

3 eggs

1½ cups milk

½ cup maple-flavored pancake syrup

1 teaspoon vanilla

2 tablespoons sugar

1 teaspoon ground cinnamon

Additional maple-flavored pancake syrup (optional)

Spray 11×7-inch baking dish with nonstick cooking spray.

Place bread cubes in even layer in prepared dish; sprinkle raisins and cream cheese evenly over bread.

Beat eggs in medium bowl with electric mixer at medium speed until blended. Add milk, ½ cup pancake syrup and vanilla; mix well. Pour egg mixture evenly over bread mixture. Cover; refrigerate at least 4 hours or overnight.

Preheat oven to 350°F. Combine sugar and cinnamon in small bowl; sprinkle evenly over strata.

Bake, uncovered, 40 to 45 minutes or until puffed, golden brown and knife inserted in center comes out clean. Cut into squares and serve with additional pancake syrup, if desired.

Makes 6 servings

personal touch

FOR A PRACTICAL AND BEAUTIFUL CENTERPIECE ON YOUR BREAKFAST TABLE, FILL A GLASS TRIFLE DISH WITH FRESH FRUIT COMPOTE. BE SURE TO CHOOSE FRUIT WITH DIFFERENT COLORS AND SHAPES.

French Toast Strata

Spinach Sensation

½ **pound bacon slices**

1 **cup (8 ounces) sour cream**

3 **eggs, separated**

2 **tablespoons all-purpose flour**

⅛ **teaspoon black pepper**

1 **package (10 ounces) frozen chopped spinach, thawed and squeezed dry**

½ **cup (2 ounces) shredded sharp Cheddar cheese**

½ **cup dry bread crumbs**

1 **tablespoon margarine or butter, melted**

Preheat oven to 350°F. Spray 2-quart round baking dish with nonstick cooking spray.

Place bacon in single layer in large skillet; cook over medium heat until crisp. Remove from skillet; drain on paper towels. Crumble and set aside.

Combine sour cream, egg yolks, flour and pepper in large bowl; set aside. Beat egg whites in medium bowl with electric mixer at high speed until stiff peaks form. Stir ¼ of egg whites into sour cream mixture; fold in remaining egg whites.

Arrange half of spinach in prepared dish. Top with half of sour cream mixture. Sprinkle ¼ cup cheese over sour cream mixture. Sprinkle bacon over cheese. Repeat layers, ending with remaining ¼ cup cheese.

Combine bread crumbs and margarine in small bowl; sprinkle evenly over cheese.

Bake, uncovered, 30 to 35 minutes or until egg mixture is set. Let stand 5 minutes before serving. *Makes 6 servings*

Spinach Sensation

Sunday Morning Upside-Down Rolls

¼ cup warm water
(105°F to 115°F)

1 envelope quick-rising
yeast

¼ teaspoon sugar

1 cup scalded milk,
slightly cooled

½ cup WESSON® Canola
Oil

½ cup sugar

3 eggs, beaten

1½ teaspoons salt

4½ cups all-purpose flour

¾ cup (1½ sticks) butter,
softened

2 cups packed brown
sugar

1 cup maraschino
cherries, chopped

1 (16-ounce) jar
KNOTT'S BERRY
FARM® Light Apricot
Pineapple Preserves

Pour water into a large bowl. Sprinkle yeast, then ¼ teaspoon sugar into water; stir well. Let stand 5 to 8 minutes or until mixture is slightly foamy. Meanwhile, in a small bowl, whisk milk, Wesson® Oil, ½ cup sugar, eggs and salt until well blended. Pour milk mixture into yeast mixture; blend well. Gradually add flour to mixture; mix until smooth. Knead dough in bowl (about 5 minutes) until smooth. Add more flour if dough is sticky. Cover with towel and let rise in warm place for 30 minutes or until dough nearly doubles in size. Punch down dough once; cover.

Meanwhile, in small bowl, cream together butter and brown sugar. Spoon (be careful not to pack) 2 teaspoons of creamed sugar mixture into each of 24 muffin cups. Sprinkle maraschino cherries over creamed sugar mixture; then add 2 teaspoons Knott's® preserves to each muffin cup. Tear small pillows of dough and place on preserves, filling each muffin cup to the rim. Cover; let rise about 15 to 20 minutes. Preheat oven to 375°F. Bake for 12 to 15 minutes or until golden brown. Immediately invert rolls onto cookie sheet. *Do not remove rolls from muffin cups.* Allow a few minutes for preserves to drip down the sides. Lift muffin pans from rolls; cool 5 minutes. Remove muffins to wire rack. Serve warm.

Makes 2 dozen rolls

Sunday Morning Upside-Down Rolls

Honey-Pecan Coffee Cake

⅔ cup milk

6 tablespoons margarine or butter, softened

9 tablespoons honey, divided

2½ to 3½ cups all-purpose flour, divided

1 package active dry yeast

¾ teaspoon salt

3 eggs, divided

1¼ cups toasted coarsely chopped pecans, divided

3 tablespoons brown sugar

1½ tablespoons margarine or butter, melted

1 tablespoon ground cinnamon

1 teaspoon water

Heat milk, softened margarine and 3 tablespoons honey in small saucepan over low heat until temperature reaches 120° to 130°F. Combine 2¼ cups flour, yeast and salt in large bowl. Slowly add heated milk mixture to flour mixture. Beat 2 eggs in small bowl; add to flour mixture. Stir with rubber spatula 2 minutes or until blended. Gradually add more flour until soft but rough dough forms.

Turn out dough onto lightly floured surface. Knead 5 to 8 minutes or until smooth and elastic, adding remaining flour to prevent sticking. Shape into ball; cover with inverted bowl. Let rise in warm place 35 to 40 minutes or until increased in size by one third. Punch down dough; turn out onto lightly floured surface. Roll out into 14×8-inch rectangle using lightly floured rolling pin.

Combine 1 cup pecans, sugar, melted margarine, cinnamon and 3 tablespoons honey in small bowl. Spread evenly over dough; press gently. Starting from one long end, roll up jelly-roll style. Pinch seams lightly; turn seam side down. Flatten slightly. Twist dough 6 to 8 turns. Grease 9-inch cake pan. Place dough in pan in loose spiral starting in center and working to side. Tuck outside end under dough; pinch to seal. Loosely cover with lightly greased plastic wrap. Let rise in warm place 60 to 75 minutes or until doubled.

Preheat oven to 375°F. Place pan on cookie sheet. Beat remaining egg with 1 teaspoon water in small bowl; brush on dough. Drizzle remaining 3 tablespoons honey evenly over top; sprinkle with remaining ¼ cup pecans. Bake 40 to 45 minutes or until deep golden brown. Turn pan and tent with sheet of foil halfway through baking time to prevent burning. Remove foil for last 5 minutes of baking. Cool in pan on wire rack 5 minutes. Remove from pan. Cool completely on wire rack.   *Makes 12 servings*

Honey-Pecan Coffee Cake

Cherry Cheese Danish Ring

1 sheet (½ of a 17¼-ounce package) frozen puff pastry

3 tablespoons unsalted butter substitute, melted and divided

1 cup (4 ounces) shredded ALPINE LACE® Reduced Sodium Muenster Cheese

⅓ cup plus 2 tablespoons sifted confectioners' sugar, divided

1 large egg yolk

1 teaspoon grated lemon peel

¼ teaspoon almond extract

1 cup dried cherries or cranberries, coarsely chopped

1 cup sliced almonds (optional)

1. Preheat the oven to 375°F. Spray a baking sheet with nonstick cooking spray.

2. On a lightly floured board, pat out the dough to a 14×18-inch rectangle and brush with 2 tablespoons of the butter.

3. In the bowl of a food processor, place the cheese, the ⅓ cup of confectioners' sugar, the egg yolk, lemon peel and almond extract. Process for 15 seconds or just until blended. (Avoid overprocessing!) Spread over the dough, leaving a ½-inch border. Sprinkle evenly with the cherries.

4. Starting at one of the wide ends, roll up dough jelly-roll-style. Place dough on the baking sheet, seam-side-down, forming a 12-inch circle and pinching the ends together.

5. Using scissors, cut at 1-inch intervals from the outside of the ring toward (but not through) the center. Twist each section half a turn, allowing the filling to show. Brush the top with the remaining tablespoon of butter. Sprinkle with the almonds, if you wish.

6. Bake for 20 minutes or just until light brown. Using a large spatula, carefully slide the ring onto the rack to cool for 15 minutes, then sprinkle with the remaining 2 tablespoons of confectioners' sugar. *Makes 1 (16-inch) danish*

Bacon-Cheese Muffins

½ **pound bacon (10 to 12 slices)**

Vegetable oil

1 egg, beaten

¾ **cup milk**

1¾ **cups all-purpose flour**

¼ **cup sugar**

1 tablespoon baking powder

1 cup (4 ounces) shredded Wisconsin Cheddar cheese

½ **cup crunchy nutlike cereal nuggets**

Preheat oven to 400°F. In large skillet, cook bacon over medium-high heat until crisp. Drain, reserving drippings. If necessary, add oil to drippings to measure ⅓ cup. In small bowl, combine dripping mixture, egg and milk; set aside. Crumble bacon; set aside.

In large bowl, combine flour, sugar and baking powder. Make well in center. Add egg mixture all at once to flour mixture, stirring just until moistened. Batter should be lumpy. Fold in bacon, cheese and cereal. Spoon into greased or paper-lined 2½-inch muffin cups, filling about ¾ full. Bake 15 to 20 minutes or until golden. Remove from pan. Cool on wire rack.   *Makes 12 muffins*

Favorite recipe from Wisconsin Milk Marketing Board

Mom's Favorite Brunch Casserole

6 eggs

1 cup plain yogurt

1 cup (4 ounces) shredded Cheddar cheese

½ **teaspoon pepper**

1 cup finely chopped ham

½ **can (8 ounces) pasteurized process cheese**

1. Preheat oven to 350°F. Lightly grease 12×8-inch baking dish.

2. Combine eggs and yogurt in medium bowl; beat with wire whisk until well blended. Stir in Cheddar cheese and pepper.

3. Place ham in prepared baking dish; pour egg mixture over ham. Bake 25 to 30 minutes or until egg mixture is set. Use process cheese to write or draw on top of casserole; let stand 2 to 3 minutes or until cheese is slightly melted.   *Makes 10 servings*

Variation: Substitute 1 pound bulk pork sausage, browned and drained, for ham.

Mushroom-Herb Omelet

**1 cup EGG BEATERS®
Healthy Real Egg
Product**

**1 tablespoon chopped
fresh parsley**

**1 teaspoon finely
chopped fresh
oregano, basil or
thyme (*or* ¼
teaspoon dried)**

**2 cups sliced fresh
mushrooms**

**2 teaspoons
FLEISCHMANN'S®
Original Margarine,
divided**

In small bowl, combine Egg Beaters, parsley and oregano, basil or thyme; set aside.

In 8-inch nonstick skillet, over medium heat, sauté mushrooms in 1 teaspoon margarine until tender; set aside. In same skillet, over medium heat, melt ½ teaspoon margarine. Pour half the egg mixture into skillet. Cook, lifting edges to allow uncooked portion to flow underneath. When almost set, spoon half of mushrooms over half of omelet. Fold other half over mushrooms; slide onto serving plate. Repeat with remaining margarine, egg mixture and mushrooms. *Makes 2 servings*

Prep Time: **10 minutes**

Cook Time: **20 minutes**

Date-Nut Granola

**2 cups uncooked, old-
fashioned rolled
oats**

2 cups barley flakes

1 cup sliced almonds

⅓ cup vegetable oil

⅓ cup honey

1 teaspoon vanilla

1 cup chopped dates

1. Preheat oven to 350°F. Grease 13×9-inch baking pan.

2. Combine oats, barley flakes and almonds in large bowl; set aside.

3. Combine oil, honey and vanilla in small bowl. Pour honey mixture over oat mixture; stir well. Pour into prepared pan.

4. Bake about 25 minutes or until toasted, stirring frequently after the first 10 minutes. Stir in dates while mixture is still hot. Cool. Store tightly covered. *Makes 6 cups*

Date-Nut Granola

Hot Cross Buns

2 cups milk

¼ cup unsalted butter, softened

6½ to 7½ cups all-purpose flour, divided

2 packages active dry yeast

¼ cup sugar

2 teaspoons salt

2 eggs

2 cups raisins

½ cup powdered sugar

2 to 4 tablespoons heavy cream

1. Heat milk and butter in small saucepan over medium heat just until butter is melted. Remove from heat; cool to about 120° to 130°F. Grease two 9×5-inch loaf pans; set aside.

2. Combine 4 cups flour, yeast, sugar and salt in large bowl. Add milk mixture and eggs. Beat vigorously 2 minutes. Add remaining flour, ¼ cup at a time, until dough begins to pull away from sides of bowl.

3. Turn out dough onto lightly floured work surface; flatten slightly. Knead 10 minutes or until smooth and elastic, adding flour if necessary to prevent sticking.

4. Shape dough into a ball. Place in large lightly oiled bowl; turn dough over once to oil surface. Cover with towel; let rise in warm place about 1 hour or until doubled in bulk.

5. Turn out dough onto lightly oiled surface; divide in half. Keep remaining half covered. Knead 1 cup raisins into half of dough. Cover with towel; let rest 5 minutes.

6. Divide dough into 15 equal pieces. Form each piece into ball. Place evenly spaced in prepared pan. Cover with towel; let rise in warm place 45 minutes. Repeat with remaining dough. Preheat oven to 400°F. Bake 15 minutes or until golden brown. Immediately remove from pan; cool on wire rack 30 minutes. Combine powdered sugar and cream, 2 tablespoons at a time, in measuring cup. Add additional cream to reach desired consistency. Pour mixture in thin stream across each bun to form a cross.

Makes 30 buns

Hot Cross Buns

Blueberry Orange Muffins

1¾ cups all-purpose flour

⅓ cup sugar

2½ teaspoons baking powder

½ teaspoon baking soda

½ teaspoon salt

½ teaspoon ground cinnamon

1 egg, slightly beaten

¾ cup fat-free (skim) milk

¼ cup butter or margarine, melted and slightly cooled

3 tablespoons orange juice concentrate, thawed

1 teaspoon vanilla

¾ cup fresh or frozen blueberries, thawed

Preheat oven to 400°F. Grease muffin pan or line with paper baking cups.

Combine flour, sugar, baking powder, baking soda, salt and cinnamon in large bowl. Set aside. Beat egg, milk, butter, orange juice concentrate and vanilla in medium bowl on medium speed of electric mixer until well combined. Add milk mixture to dry ingredients. Mix lightly until dry ingredients are barely moistened (mixture will be lumpy). Add blueberries. Stir gently just until berries are evenly distributed.

Fill muffin cups ¾ full. Bake 20 to 25 minutes (25 to 30 minutes if using frozen berries) or until toothpick inserted in center comes out clean. Remove pan and allow to cool 5 minutes. Remove to wire rack. Serve warm.   *Makes 12 muffins*

personal touch

Muffins are the perfect breakfast treat to make ahead. Simply wrap and freeze. To reheat, wrap frozen muffins in foil and heat in a 350°F oven for 15 to 20 minutes. For best flavor, use frozen muffins within one month.

Blueberry Orange Muffins

Cheddar Cheese Strata

**1 pound French bread,
cut into ½- to
¾-inch slices, crusts
removed, divided**

**2 cups (8 ounces)
shredded reduced-
fat Cheddar cheese,
divided**

2 whole eggs

3 egg whites

**4 cups fat-free (skim)
milk**

**1 teaspoon grated fresh
onion**

1 teaspoon dry mustard

½ teaspoon salt

Paprika to taste

1. Spray 13×9-inch glass baking dish with nonstick cooking spray. Place half the bread slices in bottom of prepared dish, overlapping slightly if necessary. Sprinkle with 1¼ cups cheese. Place remaining bread slices on top of cheese.

2. Whisk whole eggs and egg whites in large bowl. Add milk, onion, mustard and salt; whisk until well blended. Pour evenly over bread and cheese. Cover with remaining ¾ cup cheese and sprinkle with paprika. Cover and refrigerate 1 hour or overnight.

3. Preheat oven to 350°F. Bake strata about 45 minutes or until cheese is melted and bread is golden brown. Let stand 5 minutes before serving. Garnish with red bell pepper stars and fresh Italian parsley, if desired.   *Makes 8 servings*

personal touch

CREATE A SIMPLE TABLE SETTING THAT IS APPROPRIATE FOR THE FIRST MEAL OF THE DAY. SIMPLY PLACE A ROUND PIECE OF FRUIT IN THE CENTER OF A CLOTH NAPKIN. PULL ALL FOUR CORNERS TO THE TOP AND SLIDE A NAPKIN RING OVER THE ENDS TO HOLD IT TIGHT.

Cheddar Cheese Strata

Cranberry Scones

1 ½ **cups all-purpose flour**

½ **cup oat bran**

¼ **cup plus 1 tablespoon sugar, divided**

2 **teaspoons baking powder**

½ **teaspoon baking soda**

½ **teaspoon salt**

5 **tablespoons margarine or butter**

¾ **cup dried cranberries**

⅓ **cup milk**

1 **egg**

¼ **cup sour cream**

1 **tablespoon quick or old-fashioned oats (optional)**

Preheat oven to 425°F. Combine flour, oat bran, ¼ cup sugar, baking powder, baking soda and salt in large bowl. Cut in margarine with pastry blender or 2 knives until mixture resembles fine crumbs. Stir in cranberries. Lightly beat milk and egg in small bowl. Reserve 2 tablespoons milk mixture; set aside. Stir sour cream into remaining milk mixture. Stir into flour mixture until soft dough forms.

Turn out dough onto well-floured surface. Gently knead 10 to 12 times. Roll out into 9×6-inch rectangle. Cut dough into 6 (3-inch) squares using floured knife; cut diagonally into halves, forming 12 triangles. Place 2 inches apart on ungreased baking sheets. Brush triangles with reserved milk mixture. Sprinkle with oats, if desired, and remaining 1 tablespoon sugar.

Bake 10 to 12 minutes or until golden brown. Remove from baking sheets and cool on wire racks 10 minutes. Serve warm.

Makes 12 scones

Serving Suggestion: Serve with your favorite jellies.

Cranberry Scones

Buttermilk Pancakes with Blueberry-Orange Sauce

Blueberry-Orange Sauce (recipe follows)

2 cups all-purpose flour

1 tablespoon sugar

1½ teaspoons baking powder

½ teaspoon baking soda

½ teaspoon salt

1 egg

1½ cups buttermilk

¼ cup vegetable oil

1. Prepare Blueberry-Orange Sauce. Lightly grease and preheat griddle or large skillet over medium heat.

2. Combine flour, sugar, baking powder, baking soda and salt in large bowl.

3. Beat egg in medium bowl. Gradually add buttermilk and oil, whisking until blended. Stir egg mixture into flour mixture just until moistened.

4. For each pancake, pour about ½ cup batter onto hot griddle. Cook until tops of pancakes appear dry; turn with spatula and continue cooking 2 minutes or until golden brown. Serve with Blueberry-Orange Sauce.   *Makes 6 to 8 (5-inch) pancakes*

Blueberry-Orange Sauce

2 tablespoons cornstarch

2 tablespoons cold water

½ cup orange juice

1 tablespoon grated orange peel

1 bag (16 ounces) frozen blueberries, thawed *or* 3½ to 4 cups fresh blueberries

½ cup sugar

2 tablespoons orange-flavored liqueur

Stir cornstarch into water in medium saucepan until smooth. Add orange juice and orange peel. Add blueberries, any accumulated juices and sugar to cornstarch mixture. Cook and stir over high heat until mixture comes to a boil. Reduce heat to medium-low and simmer 2 to 3 minutes (4 to 5 minutes for fresh blueberries) or until mixture thickens, stirring occasionally. Remove from heat and stir in liqueur.   *Makes 6 to 8 servings*

Buttermilk Pancakes with Blueberry-Orange Sauce

Chunky Apple Molasses Muffins

2 cups all-purpose flour

¼ cup sugar

1 tablespoon baking powder

1 teaspoon ground cinnamon

¼ teaspoon salt

1 Fuji apple, peeled, cored and finely chopped

½ cup milk

¼ cup molasses

¼ cup vegetable oil

1 large egg

1. Heat oven to 450°F. Lightly grease eight 3-inch muffin pan cups. In large bowl, combine flour, sugar, baking powder, cinnamon and salt. Add apple and stir to distribute evenly.

2. In small bowl, beat together milk, molasses, oil and egg. Stir into dry ingredients and mix just until blended. Fill muffin pan cups with batter. Bake 5 minutes, then reduce heat to 350°F and bake 12 to 15 minutes longer or until centers of muffins spring back when gently pressed. Cool in pan 5 minutes. Remove muffins from pan and cool to warm; serve. *Makes 8 (3-inch) muffins*

Favorite recipe from Washington Apple Commission

Fruit-Filled Petal Rolls

1 package BOB EVANS® Frozen White Dinner Roll Dough

¼ cup spreadable fruit or fruit pie filling

1 cup powdered sugar

1 tablespoon orange juice

Thaw dough at room temperature 45 minutes to 1 hour. Knead until smooth. Stretch dough and roll into 12-inch square. Cut into 9 (4-inch) squares. Grease muffin pan; press squares into cups so corners are standing up. Place 1 rounded teaspoon fruit filling in each cup. Allow rolls to rise according to package directions. Preheat oven to 350°F. Bake 15 minutes or until lightly browned. For glaze, combine powdered sugar and orange juice until smooth. Brush tops of rolls with glaze. Serve warm or at room temperature. *Makes 9 rolls*

Chunky Apple Molasses Muffins

casual entertaining

menu ideas

A TASTE OF ITALY

Three Mushroom Ratatouille (page 20)

Chicken Vesuvio (page 206)

Light Lemon Cauliflower (page 127)

Cappuccino Bon Bons (page 362)

Hazelnut Biscotti (page 326)

menu ideas

IMPROMPTU GATHERINGS

Philly® Pesto Spread (page 6)

Pork Chops and Stuffing Bake (page 98)

Baked Squash (page 212)

Carrot Cake with Easy Cream Cheese Frosting (page 340)

menu ideas

MEXICAN FIESTA

Bronze Nectarine Margaritas (page 26)

Guacamole (page 23)

Chicken & Black Bean Enchiladas (page 100)

Roasted Chicken and Vegetables over Wild Rice (page 105)

Salisbury Steaks with Mushroom-Wine Sauce

1 pound lean ground beef sirloin

¾ teaspoon garlic salt or seasoned salt

¼ teaspoon pepper

2 tablespoons butter *or* margarine

1 package (8 ounces) sliced button mushrooms *or* 2 packages (4 ounces each) sliced exotic mushrooms

2 tablespoons sweet vermouth or ruby port wine

1 jar (12 ounces) *or* 1 can (10½ ounces) beef gravy

1. Heat large heavy nonstick skillet over medium-high heat 3 minutes or until hot.* Meanwhile, combine ground sirloin, garlic salt and pepper; mix well. Shape mixture into four ¼-inch-thick oval patties.

2. Place patties in skillet as they are formed; cook 3 minutes per side or until browned. Transfer to plate; keep warm. Pour off any drippings.

3. Melt butter in skillet; add mushrooms and cook 2 minutes, stirring occasionally. Add vermouth; cook 1 minute. Add gravy; mix well.

4. Return meat to skillet; simmer uncovered over medium heat 3 minutes for medium or until desired doneness, turning meat and stirring sauce once.   *Makes 4 servings*

*If pan is not heavy, use medium heat.

Note: For a special touch, sprinkle steaks with chopped parsley or chives.

Prep and Cook Time: 20 minutes

Salisbury Steak with Mushroom-Wine Sauce

Creamy Chicken & Vegetables with Puff Pastry

2 whole chicken breasts, split (about 2 pounds)

1 medium onion, sliced

4 carrots, coarsely chopped, divided

4 ribs celery with leaves, cut into 1-inch pieces, divided

1 frozen puff pastry sheet, thawed

2 tablespoons butter or margarine

1 medium onion, chopped

½ pound fresh mushrooms, sliced

½ cup all-purpose flour

1 teaspoon dried basil leaves

1 teaspoon salt

¼ to ½ teaspoon white pepper

1 cup milk

1 cup frozen peas, thawed

1. To make chicken stock, place chicken, sliced onion, ⅓ of carrots and ⅓ of celery in Dutch oven. Add enough cold water to cover. Cover and bring to a boil over medium heat. Reduce heat to low. Simmer 5 to 7 minutes or until chicken is no longer pink in center.

2. Remove chicken; cool. Strain stock through large sieve lined with several layers of dampened cheesecloth; discard vegetables. Refrigerate stock; skim off any fat that forms on top. Measure 2 cups stock.

3. When chicken is cool enough to handle, remove skin and bones; discard. Cut chicken into bite-sized pieces.

4. Place remaining carrots, celery and enough water to cover in medium saucepan. Cover; bring to a boil. Reduce heat to medium-low; simmer 8 minutes or until vegetables are crisp-tender. Set aside.

5. Preheat oven to 400°F. Roll puff pastry out on lightly floured surface to 12×8-inch rectangle. Place on ungreased baking sheet; bake 15 minutes. Set aside.

6. Melt butter in large saucepan over medium-high heat. Add chopped onion and mushrooms; cook and stir 5 minutes or until tender. Stir flour, basil, salt and pepper. Slowly pour in reserved chicken stock and milk. Cook until mixture begins to boil. Cook 1 minute longer, stirring constantly.

7. Stir in reserved chicken, peas, carrots and celery. Cook until heated through. Pour mixture into 12×8-inch baking dish; top with hot puff pastry. Bake 5 minutes until puff pastry is brown. Garnish as desired.

Makes 6 servings

Creamy Chicken & Vegetables with Puff Pastry

Italian Meatballs

1½ pounds meat loaf mix* or lean ground beef

⅓ cup dry bread crumbs

⅓ cup milk

⅓ cup grated onion

¼ cup (1 ounce) freshly grated Parmesan cheese

1 egg

2 cloves garlic, minced

1½ teaspoons dried basil leaves

1 teaspoon salt

1 teaspoon dried oregano leaves

½ teaspoon rubbed sage

¼ teaspoon crushed red pepper flakes

Marinara Sauce (recipe follows)

Additional grated Parmesan cheese and hot cooked pasta (optional)

*Meat loaf mix is a combination of ground beef, pork and veal; see your meat retailer or make your own with 1 pound lean ground beef, ¼ pound ground pork and ¼ pound ground veal.

Preheat oven to 400°F. Spray broiler pan with nonstick cooking spray. Combine all ingredients except Marinara Sauce, additional cheese and pasta in large bowl. Mix lightly but thoroughly. Shape to form meatballs using ⅓ cup meat mixture for each meatball. Place meatballs on prepared pan; bake 25 to 30 minutes until instant-read thermometer inserted into meatballs registers 145°F.

Meanwhile, prepare Marinara Sauce. Add cooked meatballs to Marinara Sauce; simmer, uncovered, about 10 minutes or until meatballs are cooked through and no longer pink in centers, turning meatballs in sauce once. (Internal temperature should register 160° to 165°F.) Serve meatballs in shallow bowls; top with sauce. Serve with cheese and pasta. Garnish as desired.

Makes 5 to 6 servings

Marinara Sauce

1½ tablespoons olive oil

3 cloves garlic, minced

1 can (28 ounces) Italian plum tomatoes, undrained

¼ cup tomato paste

2 teaspoons dried basil leaves

½ teaspoon sugar

¼ teaspoon salt

¼ teaspoon red pepper flakes

Heat oil in large skillet over medium heat. Add garlic; cook and stir 3 minutes. Stir in remaining ingredients. Bring to a boil. Reduce heat to low; simmer, uncovered, 10 minutes. Makes about 3½ cups.

Italian Meatballs

Corn Bread Taco Bake

1½ pounds ground beef

1 package (about 1⅛ ounces) taco seasoning mix

½ cup water

1 can (12 ounces) whole kernel corn, drained

½ cup chopped green pepper

1 can (8 ounces) tomato sauce

1 package (8½ ounces) corn muffin mix, plus ingredients to prepare mix

1⅓ cups FRENCH'S® French Fried Onions, divided

½ cup (2 ounces) shredded Cheddar cheese

Preheat oven to 400°F. In large skillet, brown ground beef; drain. Stir in taco seasoning, water, corn, green pepper and tomato sauce; pour mixture into 2-quart casserole. In small bowl, prepare corn muffin mix according to package directions; stir in ⅔ cup French Fried Onions. Spoon corn muffin batter around edge of beef mixture. Bake, uncovered, at 400°F for 20 minutes or until corn bread is done. Top corn bread with cheese and remaining ⅔ cup onions; bake, uncovered, 1 to 3 minutes or until onions are golden brown. *Makes 6 servings*

Microwave Directions: Crumble ground beef into 12×8-inch microwave-safe dish. Cook, covered, on HIGH 4 to 6 minutes or until beef is cooked. Stir beef halfway through cooking time. Drain well. Prepare beef mixture and top with corn muffin batter as above. Cook, uncovered, on MEDIUM (50-60%) 7 to 9 minutes or until corn bread is nearly done. Rotate dish halfway through cooking time. Top corn bread with cheese and remaining ⅔ cup onions; cook, uncovered, on HIGH 1 minute or until cheese melts. Cover casserole and let stand 10 minutes. (Corn bread will finish baking during standing time.)

Spinach Quiche

1 medium leek

Water

¼ cup butter or margarine

2 cups finely chopped cooked chicken

½ package (10 ounces) frozen chopped spinach or broccoli, cooked and drained

1 unbaked ready-to-use pie crust (10 inches in diameter)

1 tablespoon all-purpose flour

1½ cups (6 ounces) shredded Swiss cheese

4 eggs

1½ cups half-and-half or evaporated milk

2 tablespoons brandy

½ teaspoon salt

¼ teaspoon black pepper

¼ teaspoon ground nutmeg

Preheat oven to 375°F. Cut leek in half lengthwise; wash and trim, leaving 2 to 3 inches of green tops intact. Cut leek halves crosswise into thin slices. Place in small saucepan; add enough water to cover. Bring to a boil over high heat; reduce heat and simmer 5 minutes. Drain; reserve leek.

Melt butter in large skillet over medium heat. Add chicken; cook until chicken is golden, about 5 minutes. Add spinach and leek to chicken mixture; cook 1 to 2 minutes longer. Remove from heat.

Spoon chicken mixture into pie crust. Sprinkle flour and cheese over chicken mixture. Combine eggs, half-and-half, brandy, salt, pepper and nutmeg in medium bowl. Pour egg mixture over cheese.

Bake 35 to 40 minutes or until knife inserted into center comes out clean. Let stand 5 minutes before serving. Serve hot or cold.

Makes 6 servings

a helping hand

THE VERSATILE QUICHE IS EXCELLENT SERVED AS A BRUNCH OR DINNER ENTREE, AS A FIRST COURSE OR AN APPETIZER. IF YOU CHOOSE TO SERVE QUICHES AS A FIRST COURSE, CUT THEM INTO WEDGES OR MAKE MINI-QUICHES FOR EASIER SERVING.

Broccoli-Filled Chicken Roulade

2 cups broccoli florets

1 tablespoon water

¼ cup fresh parsley

1 cup diced red bell pepper

4 ounces fat-free cream cheese, softened

2 tablespoons grated Parmesan cheese

2 tablespoons lemon juice

2 tablespoons olive oil

1 teaspoon paprika

¼ teaspoon salt

1 egg

½ cup nonfat (skim) milk

4 cups cornflake cereal, crushed

1 tablespoon dried basil leaves

8 boneless skinless chicken breast halves

1. Place broccoli and water in microwavable dish; cover. Microwave at HIGH 2 minutes. Let stand, covered, 2 minutes. Drain water from broccoli. Place broccoli in food processor or blender. Add parsley; process 10 seconds, scraping side of bowl if necessary. Add bell pepper, cream cheese, Parmesan cheese, lemon juice, oil, paprika and salt. Pulse 2 to 3 times or until bell pepper is minced.

2. Preheat oven to 375°F. Spray 11×7-inch baking pan with nonstick cooking spray. Lightly beat egg in small bowl. Add milk; blend well. Place cornflake crumbs in shallow bowl. Add basil; blend well.

3. Pound chicken breasts between two pieces of plastic wrap to ¼-inch thickness using flat side of meat mallet or rolling pin. Spread each chicken breast with ⅛ of the broccoli mixture, spreading to within ½ inch of edges. Roll up chicken breast from short end, tucking in sides if possible; secure with wooden picks. Dip roulades in milk mixture; roll in cornflake crumb mixture. Place in prepared baking pan. Bake 20 minutes or until chicken is no longer pink in center and juices run clear. Garnish, if desired.

Makes 8 servings

Broccoli-Filled Chicken Roulade

Slim Walnut-Raisin Chops

½ cup orange juice

⅓ cup cider vinegar

6 lean pork chops

1 tablespoon olive oil

¼ cup sherry

¼ cup golden raisins

⅓ cup chopped
California walnuts

Combine orange juice and vinegar in shallow dish; add pork chops and marinate 20 minutes. Remove pork chops, reserving liquid. Brown chops in hot oil in large skillet; remove from pan. Add sherry, raisins and reserved liquid to pan; boil until reduced by half. Add pork chops and walnuts to pan; cover and cook over low heat for 5 minutes or until done. Serve pork chops topped with pan juices. *Makes 6 servings*

Favorite recipe from Walnut Marketing Board

Baked Spinach Risotto

1 tablespoon olive oil

1 green bell pepper,
chopped

1 medium onion,
chopped

2 cloves garlic, minced

1 cup arborio rice

3 cups chopped fresh
spinach leaves

1 (14½-ounce) can
chicken broth

½ cup grated Parmesan
cheese, divided

1 tablespoon TABASCO®
brand Green Pepper
Sauce

1 teaspoon salt

Preheat oven to 400°F. Grease 1½-quart casserole. Heat oil in 10-inch skillet over medium heat. Add green bell pepper, onion and garlic; cook 5 minutes. Add rice; stir to coat well. Stir in spinach, chicken broth, ¼ cup Parmesan cheese, TABASCO® Sauce and salt. Spoon mixture into prepared baking dish. Sprinkle with remaining ¼ cup Parmesan cheese. Bake 35 to 40 minutes or until rice is tender. *Makes 4 servings*

a helping hand

NEVER RINSE RICE WHEN MAKING RISOTTO. THE STARCH IN UNWASHED RICE IS WHAT HELPS TO MAKE RISOTTOS CREAMY.

Baked Spinach Risotto

Apricot Beef with Sesame Noodles

1 pound beef, cut for stroganoff or stir-fry

3 tablespoons Dijon mustard

3 tablespoons soy sauce

2 packages (3 ounces each) uncooked ramen noodles

2 tablespoons vegetable oil

2 cups (6 ounces) snow peas

1 medium red bell pepper, cut into cubes

¾ cup apricot preserves

½ cup beef broth

3 tablespoons chopped green onions

2 tablespoons toasted sesame seeds, divided

1. Combine beef, mustard and soy sauce in medium resealable plastic food storage bag. Shake to evenly distribute marinade; refrigerate 4 hours or overnight.

2. Cook noodles according to package directions, omitting seasoning packets.

3. Heat oil in large skillet over medium-high heat until hot. Add beef with marinade; stir-fry 2 minutes. Add snow peas and bell pepper; stir-fry 2 minutes. Add noodles, preserves, broth, onions and 1 tablespoon sesame seeds. Cook 1 minute or until heated through. Top with remaining sesame seeds before serving.

Makes 4 to 6 servings

Kitchen How-To: Toast sesame seeds in a dry, heavy skillet over medium heat 2 minutes or until golden, stirring frequently.

personal touch

For a dinner party with an Asian flare, place a red tablecloth on the dining table and arrange votive candles and fortune cookies as a unique centerpiece. Feeling daring? Set chopsticks instead of forks for each place setting.

Apricot Beef with Sesame Noodles

Pork Chops & Stuffing Bake

6 (¾-inch-thick)
boneless pork loin
chops (about
1½ pounds)

¼ teaspoon salt

⅛ teaspoon black pepper

1 tablespoon vegetable
oil

1 small onion, chopped

2 ribs celery, chopped

2 Granny Smith apples,
peeled, cored and
coarsely chopped
(about 2 cups)

1 can (14½ ounces)
reduced-sodium
chicken broth

1 can (10¾ ounces)
condensed cream of
celery soup,
undiluted

¼ cup dry white wine

6 cups herb-seasoned
stuffing cubes

Preheat oven to 375°F. Spray 13×9-inch baking dish with nonstick cooking spray.

Season both sides of pork chops with salt and pepper. Heat oil in large deep skillet over medium-high heat until hot. Add chops and cook until browned on both sides, turning once. Remove chops from skillet; set aside.

Add onion and celery to same skillet. Cook and stir 3 minutes or until onion is tender. Add apples; cook and stir 1 minute. Add broth, soup and wine; mix well. Bring to a simmer; remove from heat. Stir in stuffing cubes until evenly moistened.

Pour stuffing mixture into prepared dish, spreading evenly. Place pork chops on top of stuffing; pour any accumulated juices over chops.

Cover tightly with foil and bake 30 to 40 minutes or until pork chops are juicy and barely pink in center.   *Makes 6 servings*

a helping hand

WHEN BUYING PORK, LOOK FOR MEAT THAT'S PALE PINK WITH A SMALL AMOUNT OF MARBLING. THE DARKER PINK THE FLESH, THE OLDER THE MEAT.

Pork Chop & Stuffing Bake

Chicken and Black Bean Enchiladas

2 jars (16 ounces each) mild picante sauce

¼ cup chopped fresh cilantro

2 tablespoons chili powder

1 teaspoon ground cumin

2 cups (10 ounces) chopped cooked chicken

1 can (15 ounces) black beans, rinsed and drained

1⅓ cups FRENCH'S® French Fried Onions, divided

1 package (about 10 ounces) flour tortillas (7 inches)

1 cup (4 ounces) shredded Monterey Jack cheese with jalapeño peppers

Preheat oven 350°F. Grease 15×10-inch jelly-roll baking pan. Combine picante sauce, cilantro, chili powder and cumin in large saucepan. Bring to a boil. Reduce heat to low; simmer 5 minutes.

Combine 1½ cups sauce mixture, chicken, beans and ⅔ cup French Fried Onions in medium bowl. Spoon a scant ½ cup filling over bottom third of each tortilla. Roll up tortillas enclosing filling and arrange, seam side down, in a single layer in bottom of prepared baking pan. Spoon remaining sauce evenly over tortillas.

Bake, uncovered, 20 minutes or until heated through. Sprinkle with remaining ⅔ cup onions and cheese. Bake 5 minutes or until cheese is melted and onions are golden. Serve immediately.

Makes 5 to 6 servings (4 cups sauce, 4½ cups filling)

Tip: This is a great make-ahead party dish.

Prep Time: 45 minutes

Cook Time: 25 minutes

Chicken and Black Bean Enchiladas

Simmering Fondue

1 pound medium shrimp, peeled

8 ounces beef tenderloin, cut into thin slices

8 ounces lamb loin, cut into thin slices

2 cups sliced mushrooms

2 cups sliced carrots

2 cups broccoli florets

4 cans (about 14 ounces each) reduced-sodium chicken broth

½ cup dry white wine

1 tablespoon chopped fresh parsley

1 teaspoon bottled minced garlic

½ teaspoon dried thyme leaves

½ teaspoon dried rosemary

1. Arrange shrimp, beef, lamb, mushrooms, carrots and broccoli on large serving platter or in individual bowls.

2. Combine chicken broth, wine, parsley, garlic, thyme and rosemary in large saucepan. Bring to a boil over high heat. Remove from heat. Strain broth. Transfer broth to electric wok. Return to a simmer over high heat.

3. Thread any combination shrimp, meat and vegetables onto bamboo skewer or fondue fork. Cook in broth 2 to 3 minutes.

Makes 4 servings

Prep and Cook Time: 20 minutes

personal touch

THROW A FONDUE PARTY! START WITH A CHEESE FONDUE AS AN APPETIZER. USE A VARIETY OF BREADS AS DIPPERS. FOR DESSERT HEAT CHOCOLATE AND CREAM OR A CARAMEL ICE CREAM TOPPING; HAVE YOUR GUESTS DIP POUND CAKE, ANGEL FOOD CAKE AND FRUIT.

Simmering Fondue

Spicy Manicotti

3 cups ricotta cheese

1 cup grated Parmesan cheese, divided

2 eggs, lightly beaten

2½ tablespoons chopped fresh parsley

1 teaspoon dried Italian seasoning

½ teaspoon garlic powder

½ teaspoon salt

½ teaspoon black pepper

1 pound spicy Italian sausage

1 can (28 ounces) crushed tomatoes in purée, undrained

1 jar (26 ounces) marinara or spaghetti sauce

8 ounces uncooked manicotti shells

Preheat oven to 375°F. Spray 13×9-inch baking dish with nonstick cooking spray.

Combine ricotta, ¾ cup Parmesan, eggs, parsley, Italian seasoning, garlic powder, salt and pepper in medium bowl; set aside.

Crumble sausage into large skillet; brown over medium-high heat until no longer pink, stirring to separate meat. Drain sausage on paper towels; drain fat from skillet.

Add tomatoes with juice and marinara sauce to same skillet; bring to a boil over high heat. Reduce heat to low; simmer, uncovered, 10 minutes. Pour about one third of sauce into prepared dish.

Stuff each shell with about ½ cup cheese mixture. Place in dish. Top shells with sausage; pour remaining sauce over shells.

Cover tightly with foil and bake 50 minutes to 1 hour or until noodles are cooked. Let stand 5 minutes before serving. Serve with remaining ¼ cup Parmesan.   *Makes 8 servings*

Spicy Manicotti

Stuffed Bell Peppers

3 large bell peppers, any color, seeded and cut in half lengthwise

1½ cups chopped fresh tomatoes

1 tablespoon chopped fresh cilantro

1 jalapeño pepper, seeded and chopped

1 clove garlic, finely minced

½ teaspoon dried oregano leaves, divided

¼ teaspoon ground cumin

8 ounces lean ground round

1 cup cooked brown rice

¼ cup cholesterol-free egg substitute *or* 2 egg whites

2 tablespoons finely chopped onion

¼ teaspoon salt

⅛ teaspoon black pepper

1. Preheat oven to 350°F.

2. Place steamer basket in large saucepan; add 1 inch of water, being careful not to let water touch bottom of basket. Place bell peppers in basket; cover. Bring to a boil; reduce heat to medium. Steam peppers 8 to 10 minutes or until tender, adding additional water if necessary; drain.

3. Combine tomatoes, cilantro, jalapeño pepper, garlic, ¼ teaspoon oregano and cumin in small bowl. Set aside.

4. Thoroughly combine beef, rice, egg substitute, onion, remaining ¼ teaspoon oregano, salt and black pepper in large bowl. Stir 1 cup of tomato mixture into beef mixture. Spoon filling evenly into pepper halves; place in 13×9-inch baking dish. Cover tightly with foil.

5. Bake 45 minutes or until meat is browned and vegetables are tender. Serve with remaining tomato salsa, if desired.

Makes 6 servings

a helping hand

Bell peppers come in a variety of colors, from the traditional green or red to more exotic colors, like orange, yellow, even purple or white. Scope out the produce section or a farmers' market to pick your palette of colors.

Stuffed Bell Peppers

Indian-Spiced Chicken with Wild Rice

½ **teaspoon salt**

½ **teaspoon ground cumin**

½ **teaspoon black pepper**

¼ **teaspoon ground cinnamon**

¼ **teaspoon ground turmeric**

4 **boneless skinless chicken breast halves (about 1 pound)**

2 **tablespoons olive oil**

2 **carrots, sliced**

1 **red bell pepper, chopped**

1 **rib celery, chopped**

2 **cloves garlic, minced**

1 **package (6 ounces) long grain and wild rice mix**

2 **cups reduced-sodium chicken broth**

1 **cup raisins**

¼ **cup sliced almonds**

Combine salt, cumin, black pepper, cinnamon and turmeric in small bowl. Rub spice mixture on both sides of chicken. Place chicken on plate; cover and refrigerate 30 minutes.

Preheat oven to 350°F. Spray 13×9-inch baking dish with nonstick cooking spray.

Heat oil in large skillet over medium-high heat until hot. Add chicken; cook 2 minutes per side or until browned. Remove chicken; set aside.

Place carrots, bell pepper, celery and garlic in same skillet. Cook and stir 2 minutes. Add rice; cook 5 minutes, stirring frequently. Add seasoning packet from rice mix and broth; bring to a boil over high heat. Remove from heat; stir in raisins. Pour into prepared dish; place chicken on rice mixture. Sprinkle with almonds.

Cover tightly with foil and bake 35 minutes or until chicken is no longer pink in center and rice is tender.   *Makes 4 servings*

Indian-Spiced Chicken with Wild Rice

Tamale Pie

1 tablespoon olive or vegetable oil

1 small onion, chopped

1 pound ground beef

1 envelope LIPTON® RECIPE SECRETS® Onion Soup Mix*

1 can (14½ ounces) stewed tomatoes, undrained

½ cup water

1 can (15 to 19 ounces) red kidney beans, rinsed and drained

1 package (8½ ounces) corn muffin mix

Also terrific with LIPTON® RECIPE SECRETS® Onion-Mushroom, Beefy Onion or Beefy Mushroom Soup Mix.

• Preheat oven to 400°F.

• In 12-inch skillet, heat oil over medium heat and cook onion, stirring occasionally, 3 minutes or until tender. Stir in ground beef and cook until browned.

• Stir in onion soup mix blended with tomatoes and water. Bring to a boil over high heat, stirring with spoon to crush tomatoes. Reduce heat to low and stir in beans. Simmer uncovered, stirring occasionally, 10 minutes. Turn into 2-quart casserole.

• Prepare corn muffin mix according to package directions. Spoon evenly over casserole.

• Bake uncovered 15 minutes or until corn topping is golden and filling is hot.   *Makes about 6 servings*

personal touch

FIESTA! IT'S RELATIVELY EASY TO THROW A SIMPLE SOUTH-OF-THE-BORDER FEAST. PROVIDE PLATTERS OF TORTILLA CHIPS AND SALSA OR GUACAMOLE FOR PASSING. OTHER EASY APPETIZERS ARE CUT-UP QUESADILLAS OR CORN BREAD WITH HOMEMADE HONEY BUTTER.

Tamale Pie

Chicken with Fruit and Mixed Mustards

½ cup Dijon mustard

½ cup Bavarian or other German mustard

1 tablespoon Chinese mustard

⅓ cup honey

⅓ cup light cream

4 boneless skinless chicken breast halves

½ teaspoon salt

¼ teaspoon black pepper

2 tablespoons butter

1 cup honeydew melon balls

1 cup cantaloupe balls

4 kiwifruit, peeled and sliced

¼ cup mayonnaise

Mint sprigs for garnish

1. Combine mustards, honey and cream in medium bowl. Spoon half of mustard sauce into large glass bowl. Reserve remainder in medium bowl.

2. Sprinkle chicken with salt and pepper; add to large glass bowl with mustard sauce, turning to coat with sauce. Cover; marinate in refrigerator 30 minutes.

3. Heat butter in large skillet over medium heat until foamy. Remove chicken from mustard sauce, shaking off excess. Add to skillet in single layer. Cook 10 minutes or until chicken is brown and no longer pink in center, turning once. Remove chicken. Cut chicken across grain into thin slices; set aside.

4. Arrange chicken, melon balls and kiwifruit on serving platter; set aside.

5. Place reserved mustard sauce in small saucepan. Whisk in mayonnaise. Heat thoroughly over medium heat. Drizzle some mustard sauce over chicken. Garnish, if desired. Pass remaining sauce.

Makes 4 servings

Chicken with Fruit and Mixed Mustards

Lasagna Primavera

1 (8-ounce) package
    lasagna noodles

3 carrots, cut into
    ¼-inch slices

1 cup broccoli flowerets

1 cup zucchini, cut into
    ¼-inch slices

1 crookneck squash, cut
    into ¼-inch slices

2 (10-ounce) packages
    frozen chopped
    spinach, thawed

1 (8-ounce) package
    ricotta cheese

1 (26-ounce) jar
    NEWMAN'S OWN®
    Marinara Sauce with
    Mushrooms

3 cups (12 ounces)
    shredded
    mozzerella cheese

½ cup (2 ounces) grated
    Parmesan cheese

Bring 3 quarts water to a boil in a 6-quart saucepan over high heat. Add lasagna noodles and cook 5 minutes. Add carrots; cook 2 more minutes. Add broccoli, zucchini and crookneck squash and cook the final 2 minutes or until pasta is tender. Drain well.

Squeeze liquid out of spinach. Combine spinach with ricotta cheese. In a 3-quart rectangular baking pan, spread ⅓ of the Newman's Own® Marinara Sauce with Mushrooms. Line pan with lasagna noodles. Layer ½ each of the vegetables, spinach mixture and mozzerella cheese over the noodles; top with ½ of the remaining Newman's Own® Marinara Sauce with Mushrooms. Repeat layers. Sprinkle with Parmesan cheese.

Place baking pan on 15×10-inch baking sheet which has been lined with foil. Bake, uncovered, in a 400°F oven about 30 minutes or until hot in the center. Let stand 10 minutes before serving. (Casserole may be prepared up to 2 days before baking and refrigerated, covered, until 1 hour before baking. If cold, bake for 1 hour at 350°F.)

Makes 8 servings

a helping hand

THE KEY TO A GREAT LASAGNA THAT WON'T WEIGH YOU DOWN IS TO GO EASY ON THE PASTA. TRY NOT TO LET THE NOODLES OVERLAP, AND TRIM NOODLES WHEREVER THERE'S EXCESS.

Lasagna Primavera

Thai Chicken Fettuccine Salad

3 boneless skinless chicken breast halves (about 15 ounces)

6 ounces fettuccine

1 cup salsa

¼ cup chunky peanut butter

2 tablespoons honey

2 tablespoons orange juice

1 teaspoon soy sauce

½ teaspoon ground ginger

2 tablespoons vegetable oil

Lettuce or savoy cabbage leaves (optional)

¼ cup coarsely chopped cilantro

¼ cup peanut halves

¼ cup thin red pepper strips, cut into halves

Additional salsa (optional)

1. Cut chicken into 1-inch pieces; set aside.

2. Cook pasta according to package directions; drain.

3. While pasta is cooking, combine 1 cup salsa, peanut butter, honey, orange juice, soy sauce and ginger in small saucepan. Cook and stir over low heat until blended and smooth. Reserve ¼ cup salsa mixture.

4. Place pasta in large bowl. Pour remaining salsa mixture over pasta; toss gently to coat.

5. Heat oil in large skillet over medium-high heat until hot. Cook and stir chicken in hot oil about 5 minutes until chicken is browned on the outside and no longer pink in center.

6. Add reserved salsa mixture; mix well.

7. Arrange pasta on lettuce-lined platter. Place chicken mixture on pasta. Top with cilantro, peanut halves and pepper strips.

8. Refrigerate until mixture is cooled to room temperature. Serve with additional salsa. Garnish, if desired.   *Makes 4 servings*

Thai Chicken Fettuccine Salad

Green Salad with Pears and Pecans

¼ **cup reduced-fat mayonnaise**

¼ **cup reduced-fat sour cream**

¾ **tablespoon balsamic vinegar**

1 **tablespoon olive oil**

1 **tablespoon finely minced onion**

⅛ **teaspoon black pepper**

Salt to taste

1 **bag (10 ounces) mixed salad greens**

2 **ripe pears, cored and thinly sliced**

1 **cup (4 ounces) finely shredded Swiss cheese**

½ **cup pecans, toasted**

Pomegranate seeds (optional)

Combine mayonnaise, sour cream, vinegar, oil, onion, pepper and salt in small bowl. Blend well and set aside.

Arrange greens evenly on four plates. Place pear slices around edges of plates. Sprinkle cheese and pecans over greens. Drizzle dressing evenly over salads. Garnish with pomegranate seeds, if desired.

Makes 4 servings

a helping hand

THIS SIMPLE SALAD IS ALL THE RAGE IN FINE RESTAURANTS, YET EASY TO MAKE AT HOME. TAILOR THIS SALAD BY USING FRUIT SUCH AS APPLES OR GRAPES, AND CHEESES SUCH AS FETA OR BRIE. EVEN THE PECANS CAN BE SUBSTITUTED WITH SLIVERED ALMONDS OR SUNFLOWER SEEDS.

Green Salad with Pears and Pecans

Chicken Caesar Salad

1 package BUTTERBALL® Chicken Breast Tenders

¼ cup prepared Caesar salad dressing

½ teaspoon minced garlic

6 cups torn romaine lettuce

1 large tomato, cut into wedges

1½ cups Caesar-flavored croutons

½ cup shredded Parmesan cheese

Anchovy fillets, optional

Combine chicken, salad dressing and garlic in large skillet. Cook over medium-high heat 4 to 5 minutes or until no longer pink in center, turning frequently to brown evenly. Divide romaine lettuce among 4 plates. Top with tomato and croutons. Arrange chicken tenders on top of each salad. Sprinkle with Parmesan cheese; top with anchovy fillets. Serve with additional salad dressing.

Makes 4 servings

Prep Time: 15 minutes

Campbell's® Saucy Asparagus

1 can (10¾ ounces) CAMPBELL'S® Condensed Cream of Asparagus Soup

2 tablespoons milk

1½ pounds asparagus, cut into 1-inch pieces (about 3 cups) *or* 2 packages (10 ounces each) frozen asparagus cuts

1. In medium saucepan mix soup and milk. Over medium heat, heat to a boil, stirring occasionally.

2. Add asparagus. Reduce heat to low. Cover and cook 10 minutes or until asparagus is tender, stirring occasionally.

Makes 6 servings

Prep Time: 10 minutes

Cook Time: 15 minutes

Chicken Caesar Salad

Stuffed Tomatoes

3 large ripe red tomatoes, cored

Salt

2 tablespoons olive oil, divided

1 pound BOB EVANS® Italian Roll Sausage

1 cup chopped green bell pepper

½ medium onion, finely chopped

2 cloves garlic, minced

½ cup hot milk

1 cup dried bread crumbs

1 egg, beaten

4 tablespoons chopped fresh parsley, divided

1 teaspoon dried basil leaves

1 teaspoon dried oregano leaves

Black pepper to taste

1 cup (4 ounces) shredded mozzarella cheese

¼ cup grated Parmesan cheese

With cored side up, cut each tomato in half horizontally; remove seeds. Sprinkle interior of tomatoes lightly with salt to help remove moisture. Place tomato halves, cut sides down, on paper towels to drain about 15 minutes.

Preheat oven to 350°F. Grease baking dish with 1 tablespoon olive oil. Heat remaining tablespoon olive oil in large skillet over medium heat. Add tomato halves and cook 4 minutes on each side. Remove tomatoes from skillet and place, cut sides up, in prepared baking dish. Crumble sausage into same skillet. Add bell pepper, onion and garlic; cook until sausage is browned and onion is tender. Transfer sausage mixture to medium bowl with slotted spoon. Stir in milk and bread crumbs; let cool slightly. Add egg, 2 tablespoons parsley, basil and oregano. Season with salt and black pepper to taste. Divide mixture evenly among tomato halves and bake 10 minutes. Remove from the oven; sprinkle with mozzarella cheese. Top with Parmesan cheese. Place tomatoes under broiler until cheese is melted and golden brown. Garnish with remaining 2 tablespoons parsley and serve hot. Refrigerate leftovers.

Makes 6 side-dish servings

Stuffed Tomatoes

Southwestern Couscous

½ **cup chopped green onions, divided**

2 tablespoons FLEISCHMANN'S® Original Margarine

1 can (about 14 ounces) chicken broth

1 (14½-ounce) can stewed tomatoes

1 teaspoon ground cumin

1 teaspoon chili powder

1 (10-ounce) package couscous

1 (15-ounce) can black beans, rinsed and drained

½ **cup shredded Cheddar cheese (2 ounces)**

1. Cook and stir ⅓ cup green onions in margarine in saucepan over medium heat until tender. Stir in broth, stewed tomatoes, cumin and chili powder. Heat to a boil; remove from heat.

2. Stir in couscous and beans. Cover; let stand 5 minutes. Stir couscous mixture to fluff. Spoon couscous mixture into serving bowl; sprinkle with cheese and remaining green onions. Serve hot.

Makes 6 servings

Prep Time: 20 minutes

Cook Time: 10 minutes

Total Time: 30 minutes

personal touch

THIS SPICY COUSCOUS DISH WOULD FARE WELL AS A PART OF A TAPAS PARTY. PASS THIS ALONG WITH A PLATE OF ROASTED CHICKEN, CUT INTO BITE-SIZED PIECES, GRILLED MARINATED VEGETABLES AND OTHER FINGER FOODS. VARIETY AND EASY-TO-SERVE FOODS MAKE TAPAS PARTIES SUCCESSFUL.

Italian Broccoli with Tomatoes

4 cups broccoli florets

½ cup water

½ teaspoon Italian seasoning, crushed

½ teaspoon dried parsley flakes

¼ teaspoon salt (optional)

⅛ teaspoon pepper

2 medium tomatoes, cut into wedges

½ cup shredded mozzarella cheese

Place broccoli and water in 2-quart microwavable casserole; cover. Microwave at HIGH (100% power) 5 to 8 minutes or until crisp-tender. Drain. Stir in Italian seasoning, parsley, salt, pepper and tomatoes. Microwave, uncovered, at HIGH (100% power) 2 to 4 minutes or until tomatoes are hot. Sprinkle with cheese. Microwave 1 minute or until cheese melts.   *Makes 6 servings*

Light Lemon Cauliflower

¼ cup chopped fresh parsley, divided

½ teaspoon grated lemon peel

6 cups (about 1½ pounds) cauliflower florets

1 tablespoon reduced-fat margarine

3 cloves garlic, minced

2 tablespoons fresh lemon juice

¼ cup grated Parmesan cheese

1. Place 1 tablespoon parsley, lemon peel and about 1 inch of water in large saucepan. Place cauliflower in steamer basket and place in saucepan. Bring water to a boil over medium heat. Cover and steam 14 to 16 minutes or until cauliflower is crisp-tender. Remove to large bowl; keep warm. Reserve ½ cup hot liquid.

2. Heat margarine in small saucepan over medium heat. Add garlic; cook and stir 2 to 3 minutes or until soft. Stir in lemon juice and reserved liquid.

3. Spoon lemon sauce over cauliflower. Sprinkle with remaining 3 tablespoons parsley and cheese before serving. Garnish with lemon slices, if desired.   *Makes 6 servings*

Zucchini Tomato Bake

1 pound eggplant, coarsely chopped

2 cups thinly sliced zucchini

2 cups sliced fresh mushrooms

2 teaspoons olive oil

½ cup chopped onion

½ cup chopped fresh fennel

2 cloves garlic, minced

1 can (14½ ounces) no-salt-added whole tomatoes, undrained

1 tablespoon no-salt-added tomato paste

2 teaspoons dried basil leaves

1 teaspoon sugar

1. Preheat oven to 350°F. Arrange eggplant, zucchini and mushrooms in 9-inch square baking dish.

2. Heat oil in small skillet over medium heat. Cook and stir onion, fennel and garlic 3 to 4 minutes or until onion is tender. Add tomatoes, tomato paste, basil and sugar. Cook and stir about 4 minutes or until sauce thickens.

3. Pour sauce over eggplant mixture. Cover and bake 30 minutes. Cool slightly before serving. Garnish as desired.

Makes 6 servings

a helping hand

FENNEL IS A BULBOUS, CELERYLIKE VEGETABLE WITH A MILD, SWEET ANISE FLAVOR. THE FEATHERY TOPS ARE GREAT AS A FRAGRANT GARNISH.

Zucchini Tomato Bake

Pineapple Black Bean Salad

1 DOLE® Fresh Pineapple

1 can (14 to 16 ounces) black beans, rinsed and drained

1½ cups cooked brown rice

1½ cups cubed cooked chicken breast

1 medium DOLE® Red, Yellow or Green Bell Pepper, chopped

½ cup chopped DOLE® Celery

½ cup chopped green onions

½ cup fat-free or light honey Dijon salad dressing

Cleaned and dried corn husks

Hot peppers for garnish

• Twist crown from pineapple. Cut pineapple lengthwise into quarters. Remove fruit from shell; core fruit and cut into chunks. Measure 2 cups fruit for recipe; cover and refrigerate remaining fruit for another use.

• Combine pineapple, beans, rice, chicken, bell pepper, celery and green onions in large serving bowl. Pour dressing over salad; toss to evenly coat. Serve in corn husks and garnish with peppers, if desired.

Makes 8 servings

Prep Time: 30 minutes

a helping hand

TO AVOID WASTE WHILE MAKING THIS RECIPE AND FOR AN EASY SIDE DISH, THROW THE CORN THAT WAS PURCHASED FOR ITS HUSKS ON THE GRILL FOR THE GUESTS TO ENJOY.

Pineapple Black Bean Salad

Marinated Vegetables

2 cups broccoli florets

2 cups cauliflower florets

8 ounces fresh green
   beans, cut into
   2-inch pieces

2 cups diagonally sliced
   carrots

1 cup cherry tomatoes,
   halved

½ cup chopped red
   onion

⅓ cup GREY POUPON®
   COUNTRY DIJON®
   Mustard

⅓ cup olive oil

¼ cup red wine vinegar

1 teaspoon sugar

1 teaspoon dried
   oregano leaves

¼ teaspoon coarsely
   ground black
   pepper

⅓ cup oil-packed
   sundried tomato
   strips

In large heavy pot, steam broccoli, cauliflower, green beans and carrots until tender-crisp. Rinse vegetables in cold water and drain well; place in large serving bowl. Stir in cherry tomatoes and onion.

In small bowl, whisk mustard, oil, vinegar, sugar, oregano and pepper; stir in sundried tomatoes. Pour dressing over vegetables, tossing to coat well. Chill for at least 2 hours before serving, stirring occasionally. Garnish as desired.   *Makes 6 servings*

a helping hand

START THE PARTY! SERVE A LARGE BOWL OF MARINATED VEGETABLES WITH TOOTHPICKS THAT GUESTS CAN MUNCH ON WHILE DINNER IS BEING PREPARED.

Marinated Vegetables

Wilted Spinach Mandarin

1 tablespoon oil

½ pound fresh spinach, washed and stems removed

1 cup bean sprouts

1 can (11 ounces) mandarin oranges, drained

2 tablespoons reduced-sodium soy sauce

2 tablespoons orange juice

Quartered orange slices for garnish

Heat oil in wok or large skillet over medium-high heat. To stir-fry spinach, quickly place spinach, bean sprouts and mandarin oranges in wok. Cook and stir 1 or 2 minutes just until spinach wilts. Transfer to serving dish. Heat soy sauce and orange juice in wok; pour over spinach and toss gently to coat. Garnish, if desired. Serve immediately. *Makes 4 side-dish servings*

Campbell's® Quick Lemon-Broccoli Rice

1 can (10½ ounces) CAMPBELL'S® Condensed Chicken Broth

1 cup small broccoli flowerets

1 small carrot, shredded (about ⅓ cup)

1¼ cups uncooked Minute® Original Rice

2 teaspoons lemon juice

Generous dash pepper

1. In medium saucepan over high heat, heat broth to a boil. Add broccoli and carrot. Reduce heat to low. Cover and cook 5 minutes or until vegetables are tender.

2. Stir in rice, lemon juice and pepper. Cover and remove from heat. Let stand 5 minutes. Fluff with fork. *Makes 4 servings*

Prep Time: 10 minutes

Cook Time: 15 minutes

Wilted Spinach Mandarin

backyard bashes

menu ideas

PICNIC IN THE PARK

Grilled Jalapeño Turkey Burgers
(page 156)

Plentiful "P's" Salad (page 178)

Caramel Apple Salad (page 188)

Double Chocolate Oat Cookies
(page 324)

menu ideas

DINNER AT THE SHORE

Classic Bloody Mary (page 26)

Mini Crab Cakes (page 22)

Seafood Kabobs (page 152)

Jalapeño Cole Slaw (page 170)

menu ideas

FOURTH-OF-JULY BASH

Bacon-Wrapped Bratwurst (page 144)

Tarragon Potato Salad (page 177)

Herbed Corn on the Cob (page 166)

Firecrackers (page 284)

Bacon-Wrapped Bratwurst (page 144)

Lemon-Garlic Shish Kabobs

1½ pounds well-trimmed boneless lamb leg, cubed

¼ cup olive oil

2 tablespoons fresh lemon juice

4 cloves garlic, minced

2 tablespoons chopped fresh oregano *or* 2 teaspoons dried oregano leaves

½ teaspoon salt

½ teaspoon black pepper

1 red or yellow bell pepper, cut into 1-inch pieces

1 small zucchini, cut into 1-inch pieces

1 yellow squash, cut into 1-inch pieces

1 small red onion, cut into ½-inch wedges

8 ounces large fresh button mushrooms, wiped clean and stems trimmed

Fresh oregano sprigs for garnish

1. Place lamb in large resealable plastic food storage bag. Combine oil, lemon juice, garlic, chopped oregano, salt and black pepper in glass measuring cup; pour over lamb in bag. Close bag securely; turn to coat. Marinate lamb in refrigerator 1 to 4 hours, turning once.

2. Prepare grill for direct cooking.

3. Drain lamb, reserving marinade. Alternately thread lamb, bell pepper, zucchini, yellow squash, onion and mushrooms onto 12 (10-inch) metal skewers;* brush both sides with reserved marinade.

4. Place kabobs on grid. Grill, on covered grill, over medium-hot coals 6 minutes. Turn; continue to grill, covered, 5 to 7 minutes for medium or until desired doneness is reached. Garnish, if desired. Serve hot. *Makes 6 servings (2 kabobs each)*

If using bamboo skewers, soak in cold water 10 to 15 minutes to prevent burning.

Lemon-Garlic Shish Kabobs

Spicy Beef Back Ribs

1 cup ketchup

½ cup water

1 medium onion, shredded

2 tablespoons fresh lemon juice

1 teaspoon hot pepper sauce

½ to 1 teaspoon crushed red pepper

5 pounds beef back ribs, cut into 3 to 4 rib sections

Combine ketchup, water, onion, lemon juice, pepper sauce and red pepper in small saucepan. Bring to a boil; reduce heat. Cook slowly, uncovered, 10 to 12 minutes, stirring occasionally; keep warm. Prepare grill for indirect cooking.* Place beef back ribs, meat side up, on grid centered over drip pan. Cover. Grill ribs 45 to 60 minutes or until tender, turning occasionally. Brush reserved sauce over ribs and continue grilling, covered, 10 minutes. *Makes 5 to 6 servings*

*To prepare grill for indirect cooking, arrange equal amount of briquets on each side of grill. Place aluminum foil drip pan in center between coals. Coals are ready when ash-covered, approximately 30 minutes. Make sure coals are burning equally on both sides.

Uncovered Grilling Directions: Place ribs, meat side down, in center of double-thick rectangle of heavy duty aluminum foil. Sprinkle 2 tablespoons water over rib bones. To form packets, bring two opposite sides of aluminum foil together over top of ribs. Fold edges over 3 to 4 times, pressing crease in tightly each time. (Allow some air space.) Flatten aluminum foil at both ends; crease to form triangle and fold each end over several times toward packet, pressing tightly to seal. Place packets on grid over low to medium coals. Grill 2 hours or until tender, turning packets over every ½ hour. Remove ribs from packets and place on grid. Continue grilling 10 to 20 minutes, turning once. Brush sauce over ribs; continue cooking 10 minutes.

Prep Time: 15 minutes

Cook Time: 55 minutes to 1 hour 15 minutes

Favorite recipe from National Cattlemen's Beef Association

Spicy Beef Back Ribs

Tuna Steaks with Shrimp Creole Sauce

4 tablespoons olive oil, divided

1 medium red onion, chopped

1 red or yellow bell pepper, seeded and chopped

2 stalks celery, sliced

2 cloves garlic, minced

1 can (14½ ounces) stewed tomatoes

¼ cup FRANK'S® REDHOT® Hot Sauce

¼ cup tomato paste

½ teaspoon dried thyme leaves

1 bay leaf

½ pound medium-size raw shrimp, shelled and deveined

4 tuna, swordfish or codfish steaks, cut 1 inch thick (about 1½ pounds)

Hot cooked rice (optional)

Heat 2 tablespoons oil in medium skillet over medium-high heat. Add onion, pepper, celery and garlic; cook and stir 1 minute. Stir in tomatoes, REDHOT® sauce, tomato paste, thyme and bay leaf. Bring to a boil. Reduce heat to medium-low. Cook 5 minutes, stirring often. Add shrimp; cook 3 minutes or until shrimp turn pink. Remove and discard bay leaf. Set aside shrimp sauce.

Brush both sides of fish steaks with remaining 2 tablespoons oil. Place steaks on grid. Grill over medium-high coals 10 minutes or until fish flakes easily with a fork,* turning once. Transfer to serving platter. Spoon shrimp sauce over fish. Serve with rice, if desired. Garnish as desired. *Makes 4 servings*

*Tuna becomes dry and tough if overcooked. Cook tuna until it is opaque, but still feels somewhat soft in center. Watch carefully while grilling.

Prep Time: 15 minutes

Cook Time: 20 minutes

personal touch

ADD A LITTLE SPARKLE TO YOUR OUTDOOR PARTY WITH A SPECIAL LIGHTING SCHEME. CONSIDER TEALIGHTS ON TABLES, BAMBOO TORCHES, WHITE CHRISTMAS LIGHTS DRAPED ON TREES OR HANGING LANTERNS.

Tuna Steak with Shrimp Creole Sauce

Bacon-Wrapped Bratwurst

8 links HILLSHIRE FARM® Bratwurst

2 tablespoons mustard

2 tablespoons chopped onion

2 slices Muenster cheese, each cut into 4 strips

8 slices HILLSHIRE FARM® Bacon, partially cooked and drained

Prepared barbecue sauce

8 hot dog buns, toasted

Prepare grill for cooking. Slit Bratwurst lengthwise ¾-inch deep. Evenly spread mustard inside each slit; evenly insert onion and cheese strips. Wrap each bratwurst with 1 slice Bacon; secure with toothpick. Grill 10 minutes, turning frequently and brushing with barbecue sauce. When bacon is crisp, remove toothpicks. Serve in buns.

Makes 4 servings

Steaks with Horseradish Sauce

4 ounces light cream cheese, softened

½ cup A.1.® Original or A.1.® Bold & Spicy Steak Sauce, divided

2 tablespoons prepared horseradish

2 tablespoons chopped green onion

4 (4-ounce) beef shell steaks, about 1 inch thick

In small bowl, blend cream cheese, ¼ cup steak sauce and horseradish; stir in green onion. Cover; refrigerate at least 1 hour or up to 2 days.

Grill steaks over medium heat 5 minutes on each side or to desired doneness, turning once and basting with remaining ¼ cup steak sauce. Serve steaks topped with chilled sauce.

Makes 4 servings

Sizzling Chicken Sandwiches

1 package (1.27 ounces) LAWRY'S® Spices & Seasonings for Fajitas

1 cup chunky salsa

¼ cup water

4 boneless skinless chicken breast halves (about 1 pound)

Lettuce

4 large sandwich buns

4 slices Monterey Jack cheese

Red onion slices

Avocado slices

Additional chunky salsa

In large resealable plastic bag, combine Spices & Seasonings for Fajitas, 1 cup salsa and water; mix well. Remove ½ cup marinade for basting. Add chicken; seal bag. Marinate in refrigerator at least 2 hours. Remove chicken; discard used marinade. Grill or broil chicken, 5 to 7 minutes until no longer pink and juices run clear when cut, turning once and basting often with additional ½ cup marinade. *Do not baste during last 5 minutes of cooking.* Discard any remaining marinade. Place on lettuce-lined sandwich buns. Top with cheese, onion, avocado and salsa.   *Makes 4 servings*

Serving Suggestion: Serve with tortilla chips.

a helping hand

PLAY IT SAFE! BACTERIA SUCH AS SALMONELLA THRIVE ON POULTRY AND OTHER MEATS. THEREFORE, IT IS CRITICAL THAT YOU EITHER DISCARD MARINADE USED TO MARINATE MEAT OR BRING IT TO A FULL ROLLING BOIL FOR SEVERAL MINUTES BEFORE SERVING TO KILL ANY HARMFUL BACTERIA.

Jamaican Pork Chops with Tropical Fruit Salsa

⅔ cup prepared Italian salad dressing

⅓ cup FRANK'S® REDHOT® Hot Sauce

⅓ cup lime juice

2 tablespoons brown sugar

2 teaspoons dried thyme leaves

1 teaspoon ground allspice

½ teaspoon ground nutmeg

½ teaspoon ground cinnamon

6 loin pork chops, cut 1 inch thick (about 2½ pounds)

Tropical Fruit Salsa (recipe follows)

Place salad dressing, REDHOT sauce, lime juice, sugar and seasonings in blender or food processor. Cover and process until smooth. Reserve ½ cup dressing mixture for Tropical Fruit Salsa. Place pork chops in large resealable plastic food storage bag. Pour remaining dressing mixture over chops. Seal bag and marinate in refrigerator 1 hour.

Place chops on grid, reserving dressing mixture. Grill over medium coals 30 minutes or until pork is juicy and barely pink in center, turning and basting frequently with dressing mixture. *(Do not baste during last 5 minutes of cooking.)* Serve chops with Tropical Fruit Salsa. Garnish as desired. *Makes 6 servings*

Tropical Fruit Salsa

1 cup finely chopped fresh pineapple

1 ripe mango, peeled, seeded and finely chopped

2 tablespoons finely chopped red onion

1 tablespoon minced fresh cilantro leaves

Combine pineapple, mango, onion, cilantro and reserved ½ cup dressing mixture in small bowl. Refrigerate until chilled.

Jamaican Pork Chop with Tropical Fruit Salsa

Grilled Portobello & Pepper Wraps

1 container (8 ounces) sour cream

1 teaspoon dill weed

1 teaspoon onion powder

2 tablespoons vegetable oil

1 large clove garlic, minced

2 portobello mushrooms, stems removed

1 large green bell pepper, quartered

1 large red bell pepper, quartered

6 (6-inch) flour tortillas, warmed

1. Prepare grill for direct cooking. Combine sour cream, dill and onion powder in small bowl; set aside. Combine oil and garlic in small bowl; set aside.

2. Spray grid with nonstick cooking spray. Place mushrooms and bell peppers on prepared grid. Brush lightly with oil mixture; season with salt and pepper to taste.

3. Grill over medium-hot coals 10 minutes or until peppers are crisp-tender, turning halfway through grilling time. Remove mushrooms and peppers to cutting board; cut into 1-inch slices.

4. Place on serving platter. Serve with sour cream mixture and tortillas. *Makes 4 to 6 servings*

Prep & Cook Time: 18 minutes

personal touch

THE NAME "PORTOBELLO" WAS FIRST USED IN THE 1980's TO MARKET THE HUGE, UNSIGHTLY MUSHROOM CAPS. BEFORE THIS TIME, MUSHROOM FARMERS COULDN'T SELL THEM AND THREW THEM AWAY. PORTOBELLO MUSHROOMS ARE ACTUALLY FULLY MATURE VERSIONS OF ORDINARY WHITE MUSHROOMS.

Grilled Portobello & Pepper Wraps

BBQ Pork Sandwiches

4 pounds boneless pork loin roast, fat trimmed

1 can (14½ ounces) beef broth

⅓ cup FRENCH'S® Worcestershire Sauce

⅓ cup FRANK'S® REDHOT® Hot Sauce

SAUCE

½ cup ketchup

½ cup molasses

¼ cup FRENCH'S® CLASSIC YELLOW® Mustard

¼ cup FRENCH'S® Worcestershire Sauce

2 tablespoons FRANK'S® REDHOT® Hot Sauce

SLOW COOKER DIRECTIONS

1. Place roast in bottom of slow cooker. Combine broth, ⅓ cup *each* Worcestershire and REDHOT sauce. Pour over roast. Cover and cook on high-heat setting 5 hours* or until roast is tender.

2. Meanwhile, combine ingredients for sauce in large bowl; set aside.

3. Transfer roast to large cutting board. Discard liquid. Coarsely chop roast. Stir into reserved sauce. Spoon pork mixture on large rolls. Serve with deli potato salad, if desired.

Makes 8 to 10 servings

*Or cook 10 hours on low-heat setting.

Tip: Make additional sauce and serve on the side. Great also with barbecued ribs and chops!

Prep Time: **10 minutes**

Cook Time: **5 hours**

a helping hand

SLOW COOKER RECIPES ARE PERFECT FOR PARTIES. ASSEMBLE THE MEAL, TURN ON THE SLOW COOKER AND LET IT DO THE COOKING WHILE YOU GET READY FOR THE PARTY. AT PARTY TIME, THE FOOD WILL BE READY AND WAITING.

BBQ Pork Sandwich

Seafood Kabobs

1 pound raw large shrimp, peeled and deveined

10 ounces skinless swordfish or halibut steaks, cut 1 inch thick

2 tablespoons honey mustard

2 teaspoons fresh lemon juice

8 metal skewers (12 inches long)

8 slices bacon (regular slice, not thick)

Lemon wedges and fresh herbs (optional)

1. Spray grid with nonstick cooking spray. Prepare grill for direct cooking.

2. Place shrimp in shallow glass dish. Cut swordfish into 1-inch cubes; add to dish. Combine mustard and lemon juice in small bowl. Pour over shrimp mixture; toss lightly to coat.

3. Pierce one 12-inch metal skewer through 1 end of bacon slice. Add 1 piece shrimp. Pierce skewer through bacon slice again, wrapping bacon slice around 1 side of shrimp.

4. Add 1 piece swordfish. Pierce bacon slice again, wrapping bacon around opposite side of swordfish. Continue adding seafood and wrapping with bacon, pushing ingredients to middle of skewer until end of bacon slice is reached. Repeat with 7 more skewers. Brush any remaining mustard mixture over skewers.

5. Place skewers on grid. Grill, covered, over medium heat 8 to 10 minutes or until shrimp are opaque and swordfish flakes easily when tested with fork, turning halfway through grilling time. Garnish with lemon wedges and fresh herbs, if desired.

Makes 4 servings (2 kabobs per serving)

Note: Kabobs can be prepared up to 3 hours before grilling. Cover and refrigerate until ready to grill.

Seafood Kabobs

Pita Burgers with Cucumber-Yogurt Sauce

1 pound lean ground beef

½ cup plain low-fat yogurt

⅓ cup chopped cucumber

2 teaspoons Pepper-Herb Mix, divided (recipe follows)

¼ teaspoon salt

2 pita pocket breads, halved and warmed

1 medium tomato, cut into 8 thin slices

Combine yogurt, cucumber, ½ teaspoon Pepper-Herb Mix and salt in small bowl; reserve. Shape ground beef into four ½-inch-thick patties. Sprinkle remaining 1½ teaspoons Pepper-Herb Mix over both sides of patties. Meanwhile heat large nonstick skillet over medium heat 5 minutes. Place patties in skillet and cook 6 to 8 minutes, turning once. Season with salt, if desired. To serve, place a burger in each pita half; add 2 tomato slices and yogurt sauce as desired.   *Makes 4 servings*

Pepper-Herb Mix: Combine 2 tablespoons dried basil leaves, 1 tablespoon lemon pepper, 1 tablespoon onion powder and 1½ teaspoons rubbed sage. Store, covered, in airtight container. Shake before using to blend. Makes about ⅓ cup.

Favorite recipe from North Dakota Beef Commission

Onion-Marinated Steak

2 large red onions

1 cup *plus* 2 tablespoons WISH-BONE® Italian Dressing*

1 (2- to 3-pound) boneless sirloin or London broil steak

*Also terrific with Wish-Bone® Robusto Italian or Lite Italian Dressing.

Cut 1 onion in half; refrigerate one half. Chop remaining onion to equal 1½ cups. In blender or food processor, process 1 cup Italian dressing and chopped onion until puréed.

In large, shallow nonaluminum baking dish or plastic bag, pour 1¾ cups dressing-onion marinade over steak; turn to coat. Cover, or close bag, and marinate in refrigerator, turning occasionally, 3 to 24 hours. Refrigerate remaining ½ cup marinade.

Remove steak from marinade, discarding marinade. Grill or broil steak, turning and brushing frequently with refrigerated marinade, until steak is done.

Meanwhile, in saucepan, heat remaining 2 tablespoons Italian dressing and cook remaining onion half, cut into thin rings, stirring occasionally, 4 minutes or until tender. Serve over steak.

Makes 8 servings

Grilled Chicken Taco Salad

1 can (14½ ounces) DEL MONTE® Diced Tomatoes with Garlic & Onion

⅓ cup thick and chunky salsa, hot or medium

2 tablespoons vegetable oil

2 tablespoons red wine or cider vinegar

1 large head romaine lettuce, chopped (10 to 12 cups)

4 boneless skinless chicken breast halves, grilled and cut bite size*

1 can (8 ounces) kidney beans, drained (optional)

1 cup (4 ounces) shredded sharp Cheddar cheese

3 cups broken tortilla chips

*Or, substitute 3 cups cubed cooked chicken.

1. Drain tomatoes, reserving 1 tablespoon liquid. Chop tomatoes; set aside.

2. Make dressing in small bowl by blending reserved tomato liquid, salsa, oil and vinegar.

3. Toss lettuce with tomatoes, chicken, beans and cheese in large bowl. Add dressing as desired. Add chips; toss. Season with salt and pepper, if desired. Serve immediately. Garnish, if desired.

Makes 4 servings

Tip: To add variety to the salad, add chopped avocado, sliced green onions, olives, corn, sliced radishes and chopped cilantro, as desired.

Prep Time: 15 minutes

a helping hand

SAFETY FIRST! HIGH PROTEIN OR STARCHY FOODS, SUCH AS MEATS, KIDNEY BEANS, POTATOES OR CUSTARDS, ARE IDEAL FOR SURVIVAL AND GROWTH OF HARMFUL BACTERIA. ALWAYS KEEP HOT FOODS HOT AND COLD FOODS COLD TO PREVENT ILLNESSES.

Grilled Jalapeño Turkey Burgers

1 package (1¼ pounds) BUTTERBALL® Lean Fresh Ground Turkey

¼ cup chopped green onions

2 tablespoons chopped pickled jalapeño peppers or mild green chilies

1 clove garlic, minced

1 teaspoon Worcestershire sauce

½ teaspoon salt

⅛ teaspoon black pepper

Prepare grill for medium-direct-heat cooking. Lightly spray unheated grill rack with nonstick cooking spray. Combine all ingredients in large bowl; mix well. Form into six large patties. Grill 6 minutes on each side or until meat is no longer pink in center. Serve with your favorite condiments.   *Makes 6 burgers*

Prep Time: 15 minutes

Mustard-Grilled Red Snapper

½ cup Dijon mustard

1 tablespoon red wine vinegar

1 teaspoon ground red pepper

4 red snapper fillets (about 6 ounces each)

Fresh parsley sprigs and red peppercorns (optional)

Spray grid with nonstick cooking spray. Prepare grill for direct cooking.

Combine mustard, vinegar and pepper in small bowl; mix well. Coat fish thoroughly with mustard mixture.

Place fish on grid. Grill, covered, over medium-high heat 8 minutes or until fish flakes easily when tested with fork, turning halfway through grilling time. Garnish with parsley sprigs and red peppercorns, if desired.   *Makes 4 servings*

Grilled Jalapeño Turkey Burger

Grilled Apple-Stuffed Pork Chops

5 tablespoons FRENCH'S® Deli Brown Mustard, divided

3 tablespoons honey, divided

1 cup corn bread stuffing mix

1 small McIntosh apple, peeled, cored and chopped

¼ cup minced onion

¼ cup chopped fresh parsley

4 rib pork chops, cut 1¼ inches thick (about 2 pounds)

1. Combine ¼ *cup water*, 2 tablespoons mustard and 1 tablespoon honey in medium bowl. Add stuffing mix, apple, onion and parsley; toss until crumbs are moistened. Combine remaining 3 tablespoons mustard and 2 tablespoons honey in small bowl; set aside for glaze.

2. Cut horizontal slits in pork chops, using sharp knife, to make pockets for stuffing. Spoon stuffing evenly into pockets. Secure openings with toothpicks.

3. Place pork chops on oiled grid. Grill over medium heat 40 to 45 minutes until no longer pink near bone, turning often. Baste chops with reserved glaze during last 10 minutes of cooking.

Makes 4 servings

Prep Time: 20 minutes

Cook Time: 40 minutes

personal touch

EARLY AUTUMN IS AN UNDERRATED TIME OF YEAR FOR AN OUTDOOR PARTY. DECORATE TABLES WITH EARS OF CORN, APPLES OR GOURDS. AS THE SUN IS SETTING, SERVE MUGS OF HOT TEA OR COFFEE (AND SWEATSHIRTS, IF NECESSARY), AND ALLOW GUESTS TO BE DAZZLED BY THE SUNSET.

Grilled Apple-Stuffed Pork Chop

Mesquite-Grilled Salmon Fillets

2 tablespoons olive oil

1 clove garlic, minced

2 tablespoons lemon juice

1 teaspoon grated lemon peel

½ teaspoon dried dill weed

½ teaspoon dried thyme leaves

¼ teaspoon salt

¼ teaspoon black pepper

4 salmon fillets, ¾ to 1 inch thick (about 5 ounces each)

Cover 1 cup mesquite chips with cold water; soak 20 to 30 minutes. Prepare grill for direct cooking.

Combine oil and garlic in small microwavable bowl. Microwave at HIGH 1 minute or until garlic is tender. Add lemon juice, lemon peel, dill, thyme, salt and pepper; whisk until blended. Brush skinless sides of salmon with half of lemon mixture.

Drain mesquite chips; sprinkle chips over coals. Place salmon, skin side up, on grid. Grill, covered, over medium-high heat 4 to 5 minutes; turn and brush with remaining lemon mixture. Grill 4 to 5 minutes or until salmon flakes easily when tested with fork.

Makes 4 servings

a helping hand

IT'S EASY TO CHANGE THE FLAVOR OF GRILLED FOODS WITH READILY-AVAILABLE WOOD GRILLING CHIPS. MESQUITE, HICKORY, CHERRY AND APPLE ARE MOST COMMON.

Mesquite-Grilled Salmon Fillet

Ginger Beef and Pineapple Kabobs

1 cup LAWRY'S® Thai Ginger Marinade with Lime Juice, divided

1 can (16 ounces) pineapple chunks, juice reserved

1½ pounds sirloin steak, cut into 1½-inch cubes

2 red bell peppers, cut into chunks

2 medium onions, cut into wedges

Skewers

In large resealable plastic food storage bag, combine ½ cup Thai Ginger Marinade and 1 tablespoon pineapple juice; mix well. Add steak, bell peppers and onions; seal bag. Marinate in refrigerator at least 30 minutes. Remove steak and vegetables; discard used marinade. Alternately thread steak, vegetables and pineapple onto skewers. Grill or broil skewers 10 to 12 minutes or until desired doneness, turning once and basting often with additional ½ cup Thai Ginger Marinade. *Do not baste during last 5 minutes of cooking.* Discard any remaining marinade.   *Makes 6 servings*

Serving Suggestion: Serve kabobs with a light salad and bread.

Grilled Steak and Pepper Sandwiches

1 (1-pound) beef top round steak

¾ cup A.1.® Steak Sauce, divided

2 bell peppers (1 red and 1 green), sliced

4 large hard rolls, split and grilled

4 ounces thinly sliced mozzarella cheese

Place steak in nonmetal dish; coat with ¼ cup steak sauce. Cover; chill 1 hour, turning occasionally.

In medium skillet, over medium heat, cook and stir peppers in remaining steak sauce until tender-crisp, about 10 minutes; keep warm.

Remove steak from marinade. Grill over medium heat 6 minutes on each side or until done. Thinly slice steak; arrange on roll bottoms. Top each with warm pepper sauce, cheese slice and roll top; serve immediately.   *Makes 4 servings*

Ginger Beef and Pineapple Kabobs

South-of-the-Border "Baked" Beans

½ cup KARO® Light or Dark Corn Syrup

¼ cup ketchup

1 tablespoon cider vinegar

1 teaspoon chili powder

½ teaspoon salt

2 cans (16 ounces each) kidney or black beans, rinsed and drained

1 can (12 ounces) kernel corn, drained

1 can (4 ounces) chopped green chilies, drained, *or* 1 tablespoon seeded, chopped jalapeño pepper*

½ cup finely chopped onion

*Wear rubber gloves when working with hot peppers or wash hands in warm soapy water after handling. Avoid touching face or eyes.

1. In 1½-quart microwavable casserole combine corn syrup, ketchup, vinegar, chili powder and salt. Stir in beans, corn, chilies and onion.

2. Microwave on HIGH (100%), 15 minutes or until hot and bubbly, stirring twice. Let stand 5 minutes before serving.

Makes 6 servings

Prep Time: 35 minutes

personal touch

JUST ABOUT ANY IDEA CAN BE TRANSFORMED INTO A THEME PARTY. THROW AN ICE CREAM POTLUCK DURING THE DOG DAYS OF SUMMER TO BEAT THE HEAT. ASSIGN GUESTS TO BRING ICE CREAM, TOPPING OR CONES, AND LET IMAGINATIONS RUN WILD.

South-of-the-Border "Baked" Beans

Herbed Corn on the Cob

1 tablespoon butter or margarine

1 teaspoon mixed dried herb leaves, such as basil, oregano, sage and rosemary

⅛ teaspoon salt

Black pepper

4 ears corn, husks removed

1. Combine butter, herbs, salt and pepper in small microwavable bowl. Microwave at MEDIUM (50%) 30 to 45 seconds or until butter is melted.

2. With a pastry brush, coat corn with butter mixture. Place corn on microwavable plate; microwave at HIGH 5 to 6 minutes. Turn corn over and microwave at HIGH 5 to 6 minutes until tender.

Makes 4 servings

White Bean Salad with Cilantro Vinaigrette

1 medium red bell pepper

6 green onions with tops

2 cans (15 ounces each) Great Northern beans, rinsed and drained

½ cup prepared fat-free Italian salad dressing

2 tablespoons white wine vinegar

1 tablespoon dried cilantro

2 teaspoons sugar

2 teaspoons olive oil

Cut bell pepper into ¼-inch strips. Cut green onions into ¼-inch slices. Combine bell pepper, green onions, beans, Italian dressing, vinegar, cilantro, sugar and oil in medium bowl. Cover; refrigerate 2 hours or overnight. Garnish with purple kale and fresh cilantro, if desired.

Makes 8 servings

Herbed Corn on the Cob

Grilled Stuffed Eggplant

4 baby eggplants (1½ pounds)*

2 tablespoons olive oil

4 ounces small mushrooms, wiped clean and quartered (about 1 cup)

½ cup finely chopped green and/or red bell pepper

2 cloves garlic, minced

1 cup chunky-style salsa

1⅓ cups FRENCH'S® French Fried Onions, divided

2 tablespoons crumbled goat cheese

1 tablespoon grated Parmesan cheese

You may substitute 2 medium eggplants (1½ pounds) for the baby eggplant. Cut eggplants in half lengthwise; proceed as directed.

Cut lengthwise slice ½ inch from top of each eggplant; discard. Using a spoon or melon baller, scoop out pulp leaving ¼-inch shell. Set aside eggplant shells. Finely chop pulp.

Heat oil in large skillet over high heat. Add eggplant pulp and mushrooms; cook about 5 minutes or until liquid is evaporated, stirring often. Add pepper and garlic; cook and stir until pepper is tender. Stir in salsa. Bring to a boil. Reduce heat to medium. Cook and stir 2 minutes. Stir in ⅔ cup French Fried Onions. Spoon filling into shells, mounding slightly. Sprinkle remaining ⅔ cup onions and cheeses on top.

Place eggplant on oiled grid. Grill over medium coals 15 minutes or until eggplant shells are tender. Serve warm.

Makes 4 side-dish servings

Prep Time: 15 minutes

Cook Time: 30 minutes

Grilled Stuffed Eggplant

Jalapeño Cole Slaw

6 cups preshredded cabbage or coleslaw mix

2 tomatoes, seeded and chopped

6 green onions, coarsely chopped

2 jalapeño peppers,* finely chopped

¼ cup cider vinegar

3 tablespoons honey

1 teaspoon salt

*Jalapeño peppers can sting and irritate the skin. Wear rubber gloves when handling peppers and do not touch eyes. Wash hands after handling peppers.

1. Combine cabbage, tomatoes, green onions, jalapeños, vinegar, honey and salt in serving bowl; mix well. Cover and chill at least 2 hours before serving.

2. Stir well immediately before serving. *Makes 4 servings*

Cook's Tip: For a milder cole slaw, discard the seeds and veins when chopping the jalapeños, as this is where much of the heat of the peppers is stored.

personal touch

PLANNING A PICNIC? WRITE A COMPLETE LIST OF ALL FOODS AND EQUIPMENT TO BE PACKED. THAT WAY, THERE IS NO LAST-MINUTE SCRAMBLING AROUND OR FORGOTTEN ITEMS. DON'T OVERLOOK THE OBVIOUS, LIKE MATCHES OR SUNSCREEN, WHEN COMPILING THE LIST. OFTEN THE MOST SIMPLE ITEMS ARE MISSED THE MOST WHEN FORGOTTEN.

Jalapeño Cole Slaw

Kielbasa Tomato Salad

1 pound BOB EVANS FARMS® Kielbasa Sausage

1 pound tomatoes, cut into wedges

1 large red onion, chopped

1 red bell pepper, chopped

1 yellow bell pepper, chopped

3 green onions with tops, cut into ½-inch pieces

½ cup chopped fresh parsley

⅓ cup balsamic vinegar

2 teaspoons salt

1 teaspoon chopped fresh rosemary

1 teaspoon chopped fresh thyme

1 teaspoon black pepper

½ cup olive oil

Fresh rosemary sprig (optional)

Cut sausage kielbasa into ½-inch rounds; place in medium skillet. Cook over medium heat until browned, turning occasionally. Remove sausage to large glass bowl. Add tomatoes, red onion, bell peppers and green onions to sausage; toss lightly. Combine all remaining ingredients except oil and rosemary sprig in small bowl. Whisk in oil gradually until well blended. Pour over sausage mixture; cover and refrigerate 2 hours or until chilled. Garnish with rosemary sprig, if desired. Serve cold. Refrigerate leftovers.

Makes 8 side-dish servings

a helping hand

DUE TO ITS TOUGH TEXTURE, IT MAY BE EASIER TO CRUSH FRESH OR DRIED ROSEMARY WITH MORTAR AND PESTLE THAN TO TRY TO CHOP IT WITH A KNIFE. CRUSH OR CHOP ROSEMARY JUST BEFORE USING FOR MAXIMUM FLAVOR.

Kielbasa Tomato Salad

Grilled Vegetables & Brown Rice

1 medium zucchini

1 medium red or yellow
    bell pepper,
    quartered
    lengthwise

1 small onion, cut
    crosswise into
    1-inch-thick slices

¾ cup Italian dressing

4 cups hot cooked
    UNCLE BEN'S®
    Brown Rice

1. Cut zucchini lengthwise into thirds. Place all vegetables in large resealable plastic food storage bag; add dressing. Seal bag; refrigerate several hours or overnight.

2. Remove vegetables from marinade, reserving marinade. Place bell peppers and onion on grill over medium coals; brush with marinade. Grill 5 minutes. Turn vegetables over; add zucchini. Brush with marinade. Continue grilling until vegetables are crisp-tender, about 5 minutes, turning zucchini over after 3 minutes.

3. Remove vegetables from grill; coarsely chop. Add to hot rice; mix lightly. Season with salt and black pepper, if desired.

Makes 6 to 8 servings

a helping hand

GRILLING ADDS A UNIQUE SMOKEY FLAVOR TO VEGETABLES AND BRINGS OUT THEIR NATURAL SWEETNESS. THE EASIEST WAY TO GRILL VEGETABLES IS TO CUT THEM INTO LARGE PIECES AND TOSS THEM IN SALAD DRESSING OR SEASONED OIL BEFORE GRILLING. SEASONED RAW VEGETABLES MAY ALSO BE WRAPPED TIGHTLY IN FOIL PACKETS AND GRILLED UNTIL TENDER.

Grilled Vegetables & Brown Rice

Carrot Raisin Salad with Citrus Dressing

¾ **cup reduced-fat sour cream**

¼ **cup fat-free (skim) milk**

1 **tablespoon honey**

1 **tablespoon orange juice concentrate**

1 **tablespoon lime juice**

Peel of 1 medium orange, grated

¼ **teaspoon salt**

8 **medium carrots, peeled and coarsely shredded (about 2 cups)**

¼ **cup raisins**

⅓ **cup chopped cashews**

Combine sour cream, milk, honey, orange juice concentrate, lime juice, orange peel and salt in small bowl. Blend well and set aside.

Combine carrots and raisins in large bowl. Pour dressing over; toss to coat. Cover and refrigerate 30 minutes. Toss again before serving. Top with cashews.

Makes 8 servings

Cob Corn in Barbecue Butter

4 **ears fresh corn, shucked**

2 **tablespoons butter or margarine, softened**

½ **teaspoon dry barbecue seasoning**

¼ **teaspoon salt**

Cherry tomato wedges and Italian parsley for garnish

1. Pour 1 inch of water into large saucepan or skillet. (Do not add salt, as it will make corn tough.) Bring to a boil over medium-high heat. Add corn; cover. Cook 4 to 7 minutes until kernels are slightly crisp when pierced with fork.*

2. Remove corn with tongs to warm serving platter. Blend butter, barbecue seasoning and salt in small bowl until smooth. Serve immediately with corn. Garnish, if desired.

Makes 4 side-dish servings

Length of cooking time depends on size and age of corn.

Tarragon Potato Salad

6 medium red potatoes (about 1¾ pounds), unpeeled and scrubbed

1 cup frozen peas, thawed

¾ cup chopped green bell pepper

¾ cup reduced-fat mayonnaise

¼ cup reduced-fat (2%) milk

¼ cup sliced green onions

2 tablespoons chopped parsley

1 tablespoon lemon juice

2 teaspoons dried tarragon leaves

½ teaspoon salt

¼ teaspoon black pepper

Assorted salad greens

Place potatoes in saucepan large enough to hold them in one layer. Pour in water to just cover potatoes. Bring to a boil over high heat. Reduce to a simmer. Cover and cook 25 minutes or until tender. Drain and set aside until cool.

Slice potatoes and place in large bowl. Add peas and peppers. Toss and set aside. Combine remaining ingredients except salad greens in small bowl. Blend well. Pour over vegetables. Toss gently to coat. Cover and refrigerate at least 4 hours. Serve over greens.

Makes 6 to 8 servings

a helping hand

WANT MORE GREAT RECIPES? WE'RE ON THE WEB! VISIT US TODAY AT HTTP://WWW.FBNR.COM

Plentiful "P's" Salad

4 cups fresh black-eyed peas

1½ cups uncooked rotini pasta

1 medium red bell pepper, chopped

1 medium green bell pepper, chopped

1 medium purple onion, chopped

4 slices Provolone cheese, chopped

4 slices salami or pepperoni, chopped

1 jar (4½ ounces) whole mushrooms, drained

1 jar (2 ounces) chopped pimiento, drained

2 tablespoons chopped fresh parsley

2 tablespoons dry Italian salad dressing mix

½ teaspoon salt

¼ teaspoon black pepper

½ cup wine vinegar

¼ cup sugar

¼ cup vegetable oil

1. Place peas in large saucepan. Cover with water; bring to a boil over high heat. Reduce heat to low. Simmer, covered, until peas are soft when pierced with fork, 15 to 20 minutes. Drain and set aside.

2. Cook rotini according to package directions until tender but still firm. Drain and set aside.

3. Combine black-eyed peas, pasta, bell peppers, chopped onion, Provolone cheese, salami, mushrooms, pimiento and parsley in large bowl; set aside.

4. Combine salad dressing mix, salt and black pepper in small bowl. Add vinegar and sugar; mix well. Whisk in oil.

5. Add salad dressing mixture to black-eyed pea mixture. Toss lightly until well combined. Cover; refrigerate at least 2 hours before serving. Garnish with onion slices and green herb sprigs, if desired. *Makes 12 first-course servings*

Note: Other vegetables such as cauliflower, broccoli, carrots or celery can be added.

Plentiful "P's" Salad

Rice and Bean Salad

1 can (about 14 ounces) chicken broth

2 cups uncooked instant brown rice

1 tablespoon olive oil

1 medium onion, chopped

3 cloves garlic, minced

2 medium carrots, cut into 1-inch-julienne strips

1 medium zucchini, halved lengthwise and diagonally sliced

1 can (14½ ounces) Italian-style stewed tomatoes

1 can (15½ ounces) red beans, drained

½ cup (2 ounces) grated Parmesan cheese

½ cup Italian salad dressing

¼ cup fresh basil leaves, finely chopped

1. Bring chicken broth to a boil in medium saucepan over high heat; add rice and cover. Reduce heat and cook 10 minutes or until chicken broth is absorbed. Remove from heat; set aside.

2. Heat oil in large skillet over medium-high heat. Add onion and garlic; cook and stir 2 to 3 minutes or until onion is tender. Add carrots and zucchini; cook and stir 3 to 4 minutes or until vegetables are crisp-tender. Remove from heat. Add tomatoes, beans and rice; stir to combine.

3. Place rice mixture in large bowl. Cover with plastic wrap and refrigerate overnight.

4. To complete recipe, add Parmesan cheese, salad dressing and basil to rice mixture; toss lightly. Season to taste with black pepper. *Makes 6 servings*

Serving Suggestion: Serve with flaky breadsticks or croissants and juicy chunks of watermelon.

Make-Ahead Time: Up to 2 days before serving

Final Prep Time: 5 minutes

Rice and Bean Salad

Grilled Vegetables

¼ cup minced fresh
   herbs, such as
   parsley, thyme,
   rosemary, oregano
   or basil

1 small eggplant (about
   ¾ pound), cut into
   ¼-inch-thick slices

½ teaspoon salt

   Nonstick cooking
   spray

1 each red, green and
   yellow bell pepper,
   quartered and
   seeded

2 zucchini, cut
   lengthwise into
   ¼-inch-thick slices

1 fennel bulb, cut
   lengthwise into
   ¼-inch-thick slices

1. Combine herbs of your choice in small bowl; let stand 3 hours or overnight.

2. Place eggplant in large colander over bowl; sprinkle with salt. Drain 1 hour.

3. Heat grill until coals are glowing red. Spray vegetables with cooking spray and sprinkle with herb mixture. Grill 10 to 15 minutes or until fork-tender and lightly browned on both sides. (Cooking times vary depending on vegetable; remove vegetables as they are done to avoid overcooking.) *Makes 6 servings*

Variation: Cut vegetables into 1-inch cubes and thread onto skewers. Spray with cooking spray and sprinkle with herb mixture. Grill as directed above.

a helping hand

EGGPLANTS BECOME BITTER WITH AGE AND ARE VERY PERISHABLE. STORE THEM IN A COOL, DRY PLACE AND USE THEM WITHIN A DAY OR TWO OF PURCHASE.

Grilled Vegetables

Wild Rice & Pepper Salad

1 6-ounce package long-grain & wild rice

½ cup MIRACLE WHIP® Salad Dressing

2 tablespoons olive oil

½ teaspoon black pepper

¼ teaspoon grated lemon peel

1 cup chopped red pepper

1 cup chopped yellow pepper

¼ cup 1-inch green onion pieces

Prepare rice as directed on package, omitting margarine. Cool. Combine salad dressing, oil, black pepper and peel; mix well. Add remaining ingredients; mix lightly. Serve at room temperature or chilled.

Makes 6 servings

Substitute MIRACLE WHIP® LIGHT Reduced Calorie Salad Dressing for regular Salad Dressing.

Prep Time: 35 minutes

a helping hand

AVOID PUCKERING UP: BE SURE TO GRATE ONLY THE YELLOW PART OF A LEMON PEEL; THE WHITE PITH IS QUITE BITTER. RINSE LEMONS THOROUGHLY BEFORE GRATING THE PEEL.

Layered Orange Pineapple Mold

**1 can (20 ounces)
crushed pineapple
in juice, undrained**

Cold water

1½ cups boiling water

**1 package (8-serving
size) or 2 packages
(4-serving size)
JELL-O® Brand
Orange Flavor
Gelatin Dessert**

**1 package (8 ounces)
PHILADELPHIA®
Cream Cheese,
softened**

DRAIN pineapple, reserving juice. Add cold water to juice to make 1½ cups.

STIR boiling water into gelatin in large bowl at least 2 minutes until completely dissolved. Stir in measured pineapple juice and water. Reserve 1 cup gelatin at room temperature.

STIR ½ of the crushed pineapple into remaining gelatin. Pour into 6-cup mold. Refrigerate about 2 hours or until set but not firm (gelatin should stick to finger when touched and should mound).

STIR reserved 1 cup gelatin gradually into cream cheese in medium bowl with wire whisk until smooth. Stir in remaining crushed pineapple. Pour over gelatin layer in mold.

REFRIGERATE 4 hours or until firm. Unmold. Garnish as desired.

Makes 10 servings

Prep Time: **20 minutes**

Refrigeration Time: **6 hours**

Avocado Raspberry Spice Salad

¼ **cup seedless raspberry jam**

3 **tablespoons vegetable oil**

2½ **tablespoons white wine vinegar**

¾ **teaspoon LAWRY'S® Lemon Pepper**

¾ **teaspoon LAWRY'S® Seasoned Salt**

2½ **cups shredded napa cabbage**

1½ **cups shredded red cabbage**

2 **medium tomatoes, cut into wedges**

1 **avocado, cubed**

½ **medium cucumber, thinly sliced**

2 **tablespoons chopped green onion**

In container with stopper or lid, combine raspberry jam, oil, vinegar, Lemon Pepper and Seasoned Salt; mix well. On 4 individual serving plates, arrange napa and red cabbage. Decoratively arrange tomatoes, avocado and cucumber on top. Sprinkle with green onion. Drizzle dressing over each serving.

Makes 4 servings

Serving Suggestion: **Serve with a light French bread or croissants.**

a helping hand

TO KEEP CABBAGE CRISP FOR SALADS, STORE SHREDDED CABBAGE IN A BOWL OF ICE WATER UNTIL YOU'RE READY TO ASSEMBLE THE SALAD. DRAIN CABBAGE BEFORE USING.

Avocado Raspberry Spice Salad

Melon Salad

2½ cups boiling apple juice

1 package (8-serving size) or 2 packages (4-serving size) JELL-O® Brand Watermelon Flavor Sugar Free Low Calorie Gelatin Dessert or JELL-O® Brand Watermelon Flavor Gelatin Dessert

1½ cups cold seltzer or club soda

1 teaspoon lemon juice

2 cups cantaloupe and honeydew melon cubes

STIR boiling juice into gelatin in large bowl at least 2 minutes until completely dissolved. Stir in cold seltzer and lemon juice. Refrigerate about 1½ hours or until thickened (spoon drawn through leaves definite impression). Stir in melon cubes. Spoon into 6-cup mold.

REFRIGERATE 4 hours or until firm. Unmold. Garnish as desired.

Makes 10 servings

Prep Time: 15 minutes

Refrigeration Time: 5½ hours

Caramel Apple Salad

3 Granny Smith or other green apples, diced

3 red apples, diced

6 bars (2.07 ounces each) chocolate-covered caramel peanut nougat, chopped

1 tub (8 ounces) COOL WHIP® Whipped Topping, thawed

MIX apples and chopped candy bars in large serving bowl until well blended. Gently stir in whipped topping.

REFRIGERATE until ready to serve.   *Makes 20 servings*

Melon Salad

tried and true classics

Glazed Roast Pork Loin with Cranberry Stuffing (page 196)

Veal Piccata with Fennel

8 thin veal cutlets or veal scaloppine (about 2 ounces each)

½ teaspoon fennel seeds

Salt and freshly ground black pepper

½ cup all-purpose flour

2 tablespoons olive oil, divided

2 tablespoons butter, divided

Juice of 2 lemons

2 tablespoons white wine

2 tablespoons chopped fresh parsley

Lemon wedges for garnish

1. Pound veal with meat mallet to ⅛-inch thickness.

2. Crush fennel seeds in mortar with pestle. Or, place seeds in small resealable plastic food storage bag. Squeeze out excess air; seal bag tightly. Crush with wooden mallet.

3. Sprinkle 1 side of each veal cutlet with crushed fennel seeds; season to taste with salt and pepper. Place flour in shallow bowl. Lightly coat veal pieces with flour. (Discard leftover flour.)

4. Heat 1 tablespoon each oil and butter in large skillet over medium-high heat until butter is bubbly. Add ½ of floured veal; cook about 1 minute per side or until veal is tender. Drain well on paper towels. Repeat procedure with remaining oil, butter and floured veal. (Do not drain skillet.)

5. Combine lemon juice and wine in small bowl. To deglaze skillet, pour juice mixture into skillet. Cook over medium-high heat, scraping up any browned bits and stirring frequently.

6. Return veal to skillet; sprinkle with parsley and heat through. Transfer veal and sauce to warm serving plates. Garnish, if desired.

Makes 4 servings

Veal Piccata with Fennel

Mustard-Crusted Rib Roast

1 (3-rib) standing beef rib roast, trimmed* (6 to 7 pounds)

3 tablespoons Dijon mustard

1½ tablespoons chopped fresh tarragon *or* 1½ teaspoons dried tarragon leaves

3 cloves garlic, minced

¼ cup dry red wine

⅓ cup finely chopped shallots (about 2 shallots)

1 tablespoon all-purpose flour

1 cup beef broth

Mashed potatoes (optional)

Fresh tarragon sprigs for garnish

*Ask meat retailer to remove chine bone for easier carving. Trim fat to ¼-inch thickness.

1. Preheat oven to 450°F. Place roast, bone-side-down, in shallow roasting pan. Combine mustard, chopped tarragon and garlic in small bowl; spread over all surfaces of roast, except bottom. Insert meat thermometer into thickest part of roast, not touching bone or fat. Roast in oven 10 minutes.

2. *Reduce oven temperature to 325°F.* Roast about 20 minutes per pound or until thermometer registers 135° to 145°F for medium.

3. Transfer roast to cutting board; tent with foil. Let stand in warm place 15 minutes for easier carving.

4. To make gravy, pour fat from roasting pan, reserving 1 tablespoon in medium saucepan. Add wine to roasting pan; place over 2 burners. Cook over medium heat 2 minutes or until slightly thickened, stirring to scrape up browned bits.

5. Add shallots to drippings in saucepan; cook and stir over medium heat 4 minutes or until softened. Add flour; cook and stir 1 minute. Add broth and reserved wine mixture; cook 5 minutes or until sauce thickens, stirring occasionally. Pour through strainer into gravy boat, pressing with back of spoon on shallots; discard.

6. Serve roast with mashed potatoes and gravy. Garnish, if desired.

Makes 6 to 8 servings

Mustard-Crusted Rib Roast

Glazed Roast Pork Loin with Cranberry Stuffing

1¼ cups chopped fresh or partially thawed frozen cranberries

2 teaspoons sugar

½ cup butter or margarine

1 cup chopped onion

1 package (8 ounces) herb-seasoned stuffing mix

1 cup chicken broth

½ cup peeled and diced orange

1 egg, beaten

½ teaspoon grated orange peel

1 (2½- to 3-pound) boneless center cut loin pork roast

¼ cup currant jelly

1 tablespoon cranberry liqueur or cassis

Toss cranberries with sugar in small bowl; set aside. Melt butter in saucepan over medium heat until foamy. Add onion; cook and stir until tender. Remove from heat. Combine stuffing mix, broth, orange, egg and orange peel. Add cranberry mixture and onion; toss lightly.

Preheat oven to 325°F. To butterfly roast, cut lengthwise down roast almost to, but not through bottom. Open like a book. Cover roast with plastic wrap; pound with flat side of meat mallet. Remove plastic wrap; spread roast with part of stuffing. Close halves together and tie roast with cotton string at 2-inch intervals. Place leftover stuffing in covered casserole; bake with roast during last 45 minutes of cooking time. Place roast on meat rack in foil-lined roasting pan. Insert meat thermometer into pork.

Combine jelly and liqueur. Brush half of mixture over roast after first 45 minutes in oven. Roast 30 minutes more or until internal temperature reaches 155°F; brush with remaining jelly mixture. Transfer roast to cutting board; tent with foil. Let stand 10 to 15 minutes. Carve roast crosswise; serve with stuffing.

Makes 8 to 10 servings

Cranberry-Glazed Cornish Hens with Wild Rice

**1 box UNCLE BEN'S®
Fast Cooking Recipe
Long Grain & Wild
Rice**

½ cup sliced celery

**⅓ cup slivered almonds
(optional)**

**1 can (8 ounces) jellied
cranberry sauce,
divided**

**4 Cornish hens, thawed
(about 1 pound
each)**

**2 tablespoons olive oil,
divided**

1. Heat oven to 425°F. Prepare rice according to package directions. Stir in celery, almonds and ½ of cranberry sauce; cool.

2. Spoon about ¾ cup rice mixture into cavity of each hen. Tie drumsticks together with cotton string. Place hens, breast side up, on rack in roasting pan. Brush each hen with some of the oil. Roast 35 to 45 minutes or until juices run clear, basting occasionally with remaining oil.

3. Meanwhile, in small saucepan, heat remaining cranberry sauce until melted. Remove hens from oven; remove and discard string. Spoon cranberry sauce over hens. *Makes 4 servings*

personal touch

For place settings with a personal touch, set small photo frames at each place with a favorite picture of each guest. If you don't have photos of everybody, you can opt to write guests' names in the frames instead.

Herb-Roasted Racks of Lamb

½ **cup mango chutney, chopped**

2 to 3 cloves garlic, minced

2 whole racks (6 ribs each) lamb loin chops (2½ to 3 pounds)

1 cup fresh French or Italian bread crumbs

1 tablespoon chopped fresh thyme *or* **1 teaspoon dried thyme leaves, crushed**

1 tablespoon chopped fresh rosemary *or* **1 teaspoon dried rosemary, crushed**

1 tablespoon chopped fresh oregano *or* **1 teaspoon dried oregano**

1. Preheat oven to 400°F. Combine chutney and garlic in small bowl; spread evenly over meaty side of lamb with thin spatula. Combine remaining ingredients in separate small bowl; pat crumb mixture evenly over chutney mixture.

2. Place lamb racks, crumb sides up, on rack in shallow roasting pan. Roast in oven about 30 minutes or until instant-read thermometer inserted into lamb, but not touching bone, registers 140°F for rare or to desired doneness.

3. Place lamb on carving board. Slice between ribs into individual chops with large carving knife. Garnish with additional fresh herbs and mango slices, if desired. Serve immediately.

Makes 4 servings

a helping hand

DOMESTIC LAMB, WHICH IS FED ON GRAIN, IS MORE MILDLY FLAVORED (AND CHEAPER) THAN GRASS-FED IMPORTED LAMB.

Herb-Roasted Racks of Lamb

Crown Roast of Pork with Peach Stuffing

1 (7- to 8-pound) crown roast of pork (12 to 16 ribs)

1½ cups water

1 cup FLEISCHMANN'S® Original Margarine, divided

1 (15-ounce) package seasoned bread cubes

1 cup chopped celery

2 medium onions, chopped

1 (16-ounce) can sliced peaches, drained and chopped, reserve liquid

½ cup seedless raisins

1. Place crown roast, bone tips up, on rack in shallow roasting pan. Make a ball of foil and press into cavity to hold open. Wrap bone tips in foil. Roast at 325°F, uncovered, for 2 hours; baste with pan drippings occasionally.

2. Heat water and ¾ cup margarine in large heavy pot to a boil; remove from heat. Add bread cubes, tossing lightly with a fork; set aside.

3. Cook and stir celery and onions in remaining margarine in large skillet over medium-high heat until tender, about 5 minutes.

4. Add celery mixture, peaches with liquid and raisins to bread cube mixture, tossing to mix well.

5. Remove foil from center of roast. Spoon stuffing lightly into cavity. Roast 30 to 45 minutes more or until meat thermometer registers 155°F (internal temperature will rise to 160°F upon standing). Cover stuffing with foil, if necessary, to prevent overbrowning. Bake any remaining stuffing in greased, covered casserole during last 30 minutes of roasting.

Makes 12 to 16 servings

Prep Time: 45 minutes

Cook Time: 2 hours and 30 minutes

Total Time: 3 hours and 15 minutes

Crown Roast of Pork with Peach Stuffing

Roasted Herb & Garlic Tenderloin

1 well-trimmed beef tenderloin roast (3 to 4 pounds)

1 tablespoon black peppercorns

2 tablespoons chopped fresh basil *or* 2 teaspoons dried basil leaves, crushed

4½ teaspoons chopped fresh thyme *or* 1½ teaspoons dried thyme leaves, crushed

1 tablespoon chopped fresh rosemary *or* 1 teaspoon dried rosemary, crushed

1 tablespoon minced garlic

Salt and black pepper (optional)

1. Preheat oven to 425°F. To hold shape of roast, tie roast with cotton string in 1½-inch intervals.

2. Place peppercorns in small heavy resealable plastic food storage bag. Squeeze out excess air; seal bag tightly. Pound peppercorns with flat side of meat mallet or rolling pin until cracked.

3. Place roast on meat rack in shallow roasting pan. Combine cracked peppercorns, basil, thyme, rosemary and garlic in small bowl; rub over top surface of roast.

4. Insert meat thermometer into thickest part of roast. Roast in oven 40 to 50 minutes or until thermometer registers 125° to 130°F for rare or 135° to 145°F for medium-rare, depending on thickness of roast.

5. Transfer roast to carving board; tent with foil. Let stand 10 minutes before carving. Remove and discard string. To serve, carve crosswise into ½-inch-thick slices with large carving knife. Season with salt and pepper.   *Makes 10 to 12 servings*

Roasted Herb & Garlic Tenderloin

Holiday Turkey with Herbed Corn Bread Dressing

1 pound bulk pork sausage

1½ cups chopped onions

1 cup chopped celery

6 cups coarsely crumbled corn bread (two 8-inch squares)

⅓ cup light cream

¼ cup dry sherry

1 teaspoon dried thyme leaves

1 teaspoon dried basil leaves

1 teaspoon dried oregano leaves

½ teaspoon LAWRY'S® Garlic Powder with Parsley

1 (14- to 16-pound) turkey, thawed

LAWRY'S® Seasoned Salt

In large skillet, cook sausage until brown and crumbly; add onions and celery. Cook over medium heat 5 minutes or until tender. Add corn bread, cream, sherry, thyme, basil, oregano and Garlic Powder with Parsley. Rub cavities and outside of turkey with Seasoned Salt, using about ¼ teaspoon Seasoned Salt per pound of turkey. Pack dressing loosely into turkey cavity. Skewer opening closed. Insert meat thermometer in thickest part of breast away from bones. Place turkey, breast side up, on rack in roasting pan. Roast, uncovered, in 325°F oven 4 to 5 hours, basting frequently with melted butter or cover with foil and place on hot grill 16 to 18 minutes per pound. When internal temperature reaches 185°F, remove and let stand 20 minutes before carving. (Tent loosely with aluminum foil if turkey becomes too brown, being careful not to touch meat thermometer.) *Makes 10 servings*

Serving Suggestion: Garnish with lemon leaves and whole fresh cranberries.

personal touch

PART OF THE FORMULA FOR HAVING A SUCCESSFUL PARTY IS INVITING A GOOD BLEND OF GUESTS. TOO MANY "STAR" PERSONALITIES AT ONE PARTY CAN BE DETRIMENTAL TO GOOD CONVERSATION. A GOOD RULE OF THUMB IS TO HAVE LISTENER TYPES OUTNUMBER THE TALKERS BY ABOUT 7 TO 1.

Mustard-Crusted Roast Pork

3 tablespoons Dijon mustard

4 teaspoons minced garlic, divided

2 whole well-trimmed pork tenderloins, about 1 pound each

2 tablespoons dried thyme leaves

1 teaspoon ground black pepper

½ teaspoon salt

1 pound asparagus spears, ends trimmed

2 red or yellow bell peppers (or one of each), cut lengthwise into ½-inch-wide strips

1 cup fat-free, reduced-sodium chicken broth, divided

1. Preheat oven to 375°F. Combine mustard and 3 teaspoons garlic in small bowl. Place tenderloins on waxed paper; spread mustard mixture evenly over top and sides of both tenderloins. Combine thyme, black pepper and salt in small bowl; reserve 1 teaspoon mixture. Sprinkle remaining mixture evenly over tenderloins, patting so that seasoning adheres to mustard. Place tenderloins on rack in shallow roasting pan. Roast 25 minutes.

2. Arrange asparagus and bell peppers in single layer in shallow casserole or 13×9-inch baking pan. Add ¼ cup broth, reserved thyme mixture and remaining 1 teaspoon garlic; toss to coat.

3. Roast vegetables in oven alongside pork tenderloins 15 to 20 minutes or until thermometer inserted into center of pork registers 160°F and vegetables are tender. Transfer tenderloins to carving board; tent with foil and let stand 5 minutes. Arrange vegetables on serving platter reserving juices in dish; cover and keep warm. Add remaining ¾ cup broth and juices in dish to roasting pan. Place over range top burner(s); simmer 3 to 4 minutes over medium-high heat or until juices are reduced to ¾ cup, stirring frequently. Carve tenderloin crosswise into ¼-inch slices; arrange on serving platter. Spoon juices over tenderloin and vegetables. *Makes 8 servings*

Hickory Pork Tenderloin with Apple Topping

1¼ cups plus 2 tablespoons LAWRY'S® Hickory Marinade with Apple Cider, divided

2½ pounds pork tenderloin

1 can (1 pound, 5 ounces) apple pie filling or topping

In large resealable plastic food storage bag, combine 1 cup Hickory Marinade and tenderloin; seal bag. Marinate in refrigerator at least 30 minutes. Remove tenderloin; discard used marinade. Grill tenderloin, using indirect heat method, 35 minutes or until no longer pink in center, turning once and basting often with additional ¼ cup Hickory Marinade. Let stand 10 minutes before slicing. In medium saucepan, combine additional 2 tablespoons Hickory Marinade and apple pie filling. Cook over low heat until heated throughout. Spoon over tenderloin slices.

Makes 6 to 8 servings

Hint: Various flavored applesauces can be substituted for the apple pie filling. Try chunky applesauce with brown sugar and cinnamon.

Chicken Vesuvio

1 whole chicken (about 3¾ pounds)

¼ cup olive oil

3 tablespoons lemon juice

4 cloves garlic, minced

3 large baking potatoes

Salt and lemon pepper seasoning

Preheat oven to 375°F. Place chicken, breast side down, on rack in large shallow roasting pan. Combine olive oil, lemon juice and garlic; brush half of oil mixture over chicken. Set aside remaining oil mixture. Roast chicken, uncovered, 30 minutes.

Meanwhile, peel potatoes; cut lengthwise into quarters. Turn chicken, breast side up. Arrange potatoes around chicken in roasting pan. Brush chicken and potatoes with remaining oil mixture; sprinkle with salt and lemon pepper seasoning to taste. Roast chicken and potatoes, basting occasionally with pan juices, 50 minutes or until meat thermometer inserted into thickest part of chicken thigh, not touching bone, registers 180°F and potatoes are tender.

Makes 4 to 6 servings

Hickory Pork Tenderloin with Apple Topping

Baked Holiday Ham with Cranberry-Wine Compote

2 teaspoons peanut oil

⅔ cup chopped onion

½ cup chopped celery

1 cup red wine

1 cup honey

½ cup sugar

1 package (12 ounces) fresh cranberries

1 fully-cooked smoked ham (10 pounds)

Whole cloves

Kumquats and currant leaves for garnish

1. For Cranberry-Wine Compote, heat oil in large saucepan over medium-high heat until hot; add onion and celery. Cook until tender, stirring frequently. Stir in wine, honey and sugar; bring to a boil. Add cranberries; return to a boil. Reduce heat to low; cover and simmer 10 minutes. Cool completely.

2. Carefully ladle enough clear syrup from cranberry mixture into glass measuring cup to equal 1 cup; set aside. Transfer remaining cranberry mixture to small serving bowl; cover and refrigerate.

3. Slice away skin from ham with sharp utility knife. (Omit step if meat retailer has already removed skin.)

4. Preheat oven to 325°F. Score fat on ham in diamond design with sharp utility knife; stud with whole cloves. Place ham, fat side up, on rack in shallow roasting pan.

5. Bake, uncovered, 1½ hours. Baste ham with reserved cranberry-wine syrup. Bake 1 to 2 hours more until meat thermometer inserted into thickest part of ham, not touching bone, registers 155°F, basting with cranberry-wine syrup twice.*

6. Let ham stand 10 minutes before transferring to warm serving platter. Slice ham with large carving knife. Serve warm with chilled Cranberry-Wine Compote. Garnish, if desired.

Makes 16 to 20 servings

Total cooking time for ham should be 18 to 24 minutes per pound.

a helping hand

THE KUMQUAT IS CULTIVATED IN CHINA, JAPAN AND THE U.S. THE RIND OF THIS TINY FRUIT IS SWEET, WHILE THE FLESH INSIDE IS DRY AND TART. BOTH RIND AND FLESH CAN BE EATEN.

Baked Holiday Ham with Cranberry-Wine Compote

Swiss-Style Twice Baked Potatoes

4 large, evenly shaped baking potatoes (about 2½ pounds)

4 teaspoons butter or margarine, softened

⅔ cup grated Emmentaler cheese*

⅔ cup grated Gruyère cheese*

½ teaspoon caraway seeds (optional)

4 teaspoons dry white wine

2 teaspoons kirsch (cherry brandy)

½ teaspoon minced garlic

½ teaspoon salt

*Emmentaler and Gruyère are imported Swiss cheeses that tend to be aged longer than domestic Swiss. If unavailable, any Swiss cheese may be used.

1. Preheat oven to 425°F. Scrub potatoes. Dry well. Rub each potato with 1 teaspoon butter. Pierce potatoes several times with fork. Place in shallow baking dish at least 1 inch apart. Bake 50 to 60 minutes or until tender. Cool for several minutes.

2. Meanwhile, place cheeses and caraway seeds in small bowl. Toss well; set aside.

3. Cut off top ⅓ of potatoes. Scoop out potato pulp from bottom sections leaving ¼-inch shell. Place pulp in large bowl, reserving shells. Add pulp from potato tops to bowl; discard top skins.

4. Mash with potato masher until smooth. Add wine, kirsch, garlic and salt. Mash to blend; stir in cheese mixture. Mash lightly, just enough to blend all ingredients well. Spoon mixture into potato shells, mounding evenly.

5. Place potatoes in same baking dish. Bake 20 to 25 minutes more until tops are lightly browned and potatoes are heated through. Serve hot on decorative kale, if desired.

Makes 4 servings

Swiss-Style Twice Baked Potatoes

Baked Squash

2 medium-sized acorn squash

2 tart red apples, diced

½ cup chopped nuts

½ cup SMUCKER'S® Apple Jelly

¼ cup butter or margarine, softened

Cut squash in half crosswise or lengthwise; scoop out centers. Place in baking pan. Combine apples, nuts, jelly and butter. Fill squash with mixture. Pour a small amount of boiling water in bottom of pan around squash. Cover pan with foil.

Bake at 400°F 45 to 60 minutes or until fork-tender. Remove foil during last 5 minutes of baking. *Makes 4 servings*

Green Beans with Blue Cheese and Roasted Peppers

1 bag (20 ounces) frozen cut green beans

½ jar (about 3 ounces) roasted red pepper strips, drained and slivered

⅛ teaspoon salt

⅛ teaspoon white pepper

4 ounces cream cheese

½ cup milk

¾ cup blue cheese (3 ounces), crumbled

½ cup Italian-style bread crumbs

1 tablespoon margarine or butter, melted

Preheat oven to 350°F. Spray 2-quart oval casserole with nonstick cooking spray.

Combine green beans, red pepper strips, salt and pepper in prepared dish.

Place cream cheese and milk in small saucepan; heat over low heat, stirring until melted. Add blue cheese; stir only until combined. Pour cheese mixture over green bean mixture and stir until green beans are coated.

Combine bread crumbs and margarine in small bowl; sprinkle evenly over casserole.

Bake, uncovered, 20 minutes or until hot and bubbly.

Makes 4 servings

Green Beans with Blue Cheese and Roasted Peppers

Classic Spinach Soufflé

1 pound fresh spinach leaves

¼ cup butter or margarine

2 tablespoons finely chopped onion

¼ cup all-purpose flour

¼ teaspoon salt

¼ teaspoon ground nutmeg

⅛ teaspoon black pepper

1 cup milk

4 eggs, separated

1 cup (4 ounces) shredded sharp Cheddar cheese

1. Preheat oven to 375°F. Grease 1½- or 2-quart soufflé dish; set aside.

2. Bring 1 quart salted water in 2-quart saucepan to a boil over high heat. Add spinach. Return to a boil and cook 2 to 3 minutes or until spinach is crisp-tender. Drain spinach and immediately plunge into cold water. Drain spinach and let stand until cool enough to handle. Squeeze spinach to remove excess moisture. Finely chop spinach.

3. Melt butter in large saucepan over medium heat. Add onion; cook and stir 2 to 3 minutes. Stir in flour, salt, nutmeg and pepper. Gradually stir in milk. Cook and stir until mixture comes to a boil and thickens. Remove from heat.

4. Stir egg yolks into saucepan until well blended. Add spinach and cheese; mix well.

5. Beat egg whites in clean large bowl with electric mixer at high speed until stiff peaks form. Fold egg whites into spinach mixture until egg whites are evenly incorporated. Pour into prepared dish.

6. Bake 35 to 40 minutes or until puffed and wooden skewer inserted in center comes out clean. Garnish, if desired. Serve immediately. *Makes 4 servings*

Classic Spinach Soufflé

Roasted Mixed Vegetables

4 large red skin potatoes, cut into wedges (about 2 pounds)

3 large carrots, peeled and cut into 1½-inch pieces (about 2 cups)

3 large parsnips, peeled and cut into 1½-inch pieces (about 2 cups)

2 large onions, cut into wedges

1 tablespoon dried rosemary leaves

2 teaspoons garlic powder

¼ cup FLEISCHMANN'S® Original Margarine, melted

1. Mix potatoes, carrots, parsnips and onions with rosemary and garlic powder in large bowl.

2. Drizzle with melted margarine, tossing to coat well. Spread in a 13×9×2-inch baking pan.

3. Bake at 450°F for 40 to 45 minutes or until fork-tender, stirring occasionally.

Makes 8 servings

Prep Time: 15 minutes

Cook Time: 40 minutes

Total Time: 55 minutes

a helping hand

THE PARSNIP IS A ROOT VEGETABLE WHICH IS AVAILABLE YEAR-ROUND, BUT THE BEST TIME TO BUY THEM IS DURING THE FALL AND WINTER MONTHS, WHEN THEY ARE IN SEASON. THE FIRST FROST OF THE YEAR CONVERTS THE PARSNIP'S STARCH TO SUGAR, WHICH IMPARTS A MILD, SWEET FLAVOR.

Roasted Mixed Vegetables

Pepperidge Farm® Sausage Corn Bread Stuffing

¼ **pound bulk pork sausage**

1¼ **cups water**

½ **cup cooked whole kernel corn**

½ **cup shredded Cheddar cheese (2 ounces)**

1 **tablespoon chopped fresh parsley** *or* 1 **teaspoon dried parsley flakes**

4 **cups PEPPERIDGE FARM® Corn Bread Stuffing**

1. In large saucepan over medium-high heat, cook sausage until browned, stirring to separate meat. Pour off fat.

2. Stir in water, corn, cheese and parsley. Add stuffing. Mix lightly. Spoon into greased 1½-quart casserole.

3. Cover and bake at 350°F. for 25 minutes or until hot.

Makes 6 servings

Tip: This stuffing bake brings a new flavor to the traditional holiday meal—and is easy enough for an everyday meal!

Prep Time: 15 minutes

Cook Time: 25 minutes

Honey-Mustard Roasted Potatoes

4 **large baking potatoes (about 2 pounds)**

½ **cup Dijon mustard**

¼ **cup honey**

½ **teaspoon crushed dried thyme leaves**

Salt and black pepper to taste

Peel potatoes and cut each into 6 to 8 pieces. Cover potatoes with salted water in large saucepan. Bring to a boil over medium-high heat. Cook potatoes 12 to 15 minutes or until just tender. Drain. Combine mustard, honey and thyme in small bowl. Toss potatoes with honey-thyme mustard in large bowl until evenly coated. Arrange potatoes on foil-lined baking sheet coated with nonstick cooking spray. Bake at 375°F 20 minutes or until potatoes begin to brown around edges. Season to taste with salt and pepper.

Makes 4 servings

Favorite recipe from National Honey Board

Green Bean Bundles

8 ounces haricot vert beans or other tiny, young green beans

1 yellow squash, about 1½ inches in diameter

1 tablespoon olive oil

1 clove garlic, minced

¼ teaspoon dried tarragon leaves, crushed

Salt and black pepper

Place beans in colander; rinse well. Snap off stem end from each bean; arrange beans in 8 stacks, about 10 to 12 beans per stack. Cut eight ½-inch-thick slices of squash; hollow out with spoon to within ¼ inch of rind. Thread bean stacks through squash pieces as if each piece were a napkin ring.

Place steamer basket in large stockpot or saucepan; add 1 inch of water. (Water should not touch bottom of basket.) Place bean bundles in steamer basket. Cover. Bring to a boil over high heat; steam 4 minutes or until beans are bright green and crisp-tender. Add water, as necessary, to prevent pan from boiling dry.

Meanwhile, heat oil in small skillet over medium-high heat. Cook and stir garlic and tarragon in hot oil until garlic is soft but not brown. Transfer bean bundles to warm serving plate and pour garlic oil over top. Season to taste with salt and pepper. Garnish, if desired. Serve immediately. *Makes 8 side-dish servings*

Swanson® Garlic Mashed Potatoes

2 cans (14½ ounces *each*) SWANSON® Seasoned Chicken Broth with Roasted Garlic

5 large potatoes, cut into 1-inch pieces

1. In medium saucepan place broth and potatoes. Over high heat, heat to a boil. Reduce heat to medium. Cover and cook 10 minutes or until potatoes are tender. Drain, reserving broth.

2. Mash potatoes with *1¼ cups* reserved broth. If needed, add additional broth until potatoes are desired consistency.

Makes about 6 servings

Skinny Mashed Potatoes: Substitute 2 cans (14½ ounces *each*) SWANSON® Chicken Broth for Chicken Broth with Roasted Garlic.

Prep Time: **10 minutes**

Cook Time: **15 minutes**

Spinach & Grapefruit Salad

1 bag (10 ounces) spinach, washed, stemmed and torn

2 cups sliced mushrooms

½ of a red onion, sliced into thin wedges

6 slices uncooked bacon, cut into thin strips

2 teaspoons cornstarch

½ cup cider vinegar

3 tablespoons sugar

3 tablespoons FRENCH'S® Deli Brown Mustard

1 teaspoon FRENCH'S® Worcestershire Sauce

2 pink grapefruits, peeled and cut into sections

1. Place spinach in large salad bowl. Add mushrooms and onion; set aside. Cook bacon in large nonstick skillet over medium-high heat until bacon is crisp. Drain; reserve 2 tablespoons drippings in pan.

2. Combine ½ *cup water* and cornstarch in 2-cup measure until blended. Stir in vinegar, sugar, mustard and Worcestershire. Pour into skillet with bacon drippings. Bring to a boil; simmer 2 minutes or until thickened, whisking constantly. Cool slightly. Top salad with bacon and grapefruit. Pour dressing over salad; toss well to coat evenly. Serve immediately. *Makes 6 to 8 servings*

Prep Time: 25 minutes

Cook Time: 10 minutes

a helping hand

PARTIALLY FREEZE BACON FOR EASIER AND LESS MESSY SLICING. THIS PREVENTS RAGGED, STRETCHED PIECES OF BACON.

Spinach & Grapefruit Salad

Cherry Waldorf Salad

1¼ cups apple juice, divided

1 package (4-serving size) JELL-O® Brand Cherry Flavor Sugar Free Gelatin Dessert

Ice cubes

½ cup finely chopped peeled apple

1 small banana, sliced or finely chopped

¼ cup sliced celery

BRING ¾ cup apple juice to a boil in medium saucepan. Completely dissolve gelatin in boiling apple juice. Combine the remaining ½ cup apple juice and enough ice cubes to measure 1¼ cups. Add to gelatin; stir until slightly thickened. Remove any unmelted ice. Stir in fruit and celery. Spoon into individual dishes or medium serving bowl. Chill until firm, about 2 hours.

Makes 2½ cups or 5 servings

Sweet Potatoes with Brandy and Raisins

½ cup seedless raisins

¼ cup brandy

4 medium sweet potatoes, boiled until just tender then peeled and sliced into ¼-inch slices

⅔ cup packed brown sugar

¼ cup FLEISCHMANN'S® Original Margarine

2 tablespoons water

¼ teaspoon ground cinnamon

1. Mix raisins and brandy in bowl; let stand 20 minutes. Drain.

2. Layer sweet potatoes in 9×9×2-inch baking pan; top with raisins.

3. Mix brown sugar, margarine, water and cinnamon in small saucepan; heat to a boil. Pour over sweet potatoes.

4. Bake in preheated 350°F oven for 40 minutes, basting with pan juices occasionally.
Makes 4 to 6 servings

Prep Time: 20 minutes

Cook Time: 40 minutes

Total Time: 1 hour

Sweet Potatoes with Brandy and Raisins

222

Saucy Garden Patch Vegetables

1 can (10¾ ounces)
condensed Cheddar
cheese soup

½ cup sour cream

¼ cup milk

1 bag (16 ounces)
frozen vegetable
combination, such
as broccoli, corn
and red bell pepper,
thawed and drained

1 bag (16 ounces)
frozen vegetable
combination, such
as brussels sprouts,
carrots and
cauliflower, thawed
and drained

1 cup (4 ounces)
shredded Cheddar
cheese

1⅓ cups FRENCH'S®
French Fried
Onions, divided

Microwave Directions: Combine soup, sour cream and milk in large bowl. Stir in vegetables, cheese and ⅔ cup French Fried Onions. Spoon into microwavable 2-quart oblong baking dish.

Cover loosely with plastic wrap. Microwave on HIGH 10 minutes or until vegetables are tender and mixture is heated through, stirring halfway through cooking time. Uncover; sprinkle with remaining ⅔ cup onions. Microwave on HIGH 1 minute or until onions are golden. *Makes 8 to 10 servings*

Oven Directions: Prepare vegetable mixture as above. Bake, covered, in 400°F oven 45 minutes or until tender and mixture is heated through. Stir; sprinkle with remaining onions. Bake, uncovered, 1 minute.

Prep Time: 10 minutes

Cook Time: 11 minutes

personal touch

IT'S A WRAP! THIS EASY SIDE DISH TRAVELS WELL TO POTLUCKS. SIMPLY COOK IT IN A CASSEROLE DISH WITH A TIGHT-FITTING LID AND TRANSPORT IT TO YOUR NEXT POTLUCK FEAST.

Saucy Garden Patch Vegetables

Corn Maque Choux

2 tablespoons butter or margarine

½ cup chopped onion

½ cup chopped green pepper

4 cups whole kernel corn (canned, fresh or frozen, thawed)

1 medium tomato, chopped

¼ teaspoon salt

½ teaspoon TABASCO® brand Pepper Sauce

Melt butter over medium heat in 3-quart saucepan.

Add onion and green pepper; cook 5 minutes or until tender, stirring frequently.

Stir in corn, tomato, salt and TABASCO® Sauce.

Reduce heat and simmer 10 to 15 minutes or until corn is tender.

Makes 3 cups

Orange-Glazed Carrots

1 pound fresh or thawed frozen baby carrots

⅓ cup orange marmalade

2 tablespoons butter

2 teaspoons Dijon mustard

½ teaspoon grated fresh ginger

Heat 1 inch lightly salted water in 2-quart saucepan over high heat to a boil; add carrots. Return to a boil. Reduce heat to low. Cover and simmer 10 to 12 minutes for fresh carrots (8 to 10 minutes for frozen carrots) or until crisp-tender. Drain well; return carrots to pan. Stir in marmalade, butter, mustard and ginger. Simmer, uncovered, over medium heat 3 minutes or until carrots are glazed, stirring occasionally.*

Makes 6 servings

At this point, carrots may be transferred to a microwavable casserole dish with lid. Cover and refrigerate up to 8 hours before serving. To reheat, microwave at HIGH (100% power) 4 to 5 minutes or until hot.

Note: Recipe may be doubled.

Wild Rice and Lentil Pilaf

4½ cups water, divided

¾ cup dried brown lentils, sorted, rinsed and drained

1 tablespoon plus 2 teaspoons extra-virgin olive oil, divided

2 cups finely chopped yellow onions

1 medium red bell pepper, chopped

1 cup thinly sliced celery

4 cloves garlic, minced

½ teaspoon dried oregano leaves

½ teaspoon salt

Dash ground red pepper (optional)

1 box (6.2-ounce) quick-cooking white and wild rice with seasoning packet

Bring 4 cups water to a boil in medium saucepan. Stir in lentils and return to a boil. Reduce heat to low and simmer, uncovered, 10 minutes.

Meanwhile, heat large nonstick skillet over medium-high heat until hot. Coat skillet with nonstick cooking spray. Add 2 teaspoons oil and tilt skillet to coat bottom evenly. Add onions, bell pepper, celery, garlic and oregano; cook 12 minutes or until celery is crisp-tender, stirring frequently. Stir in remaining ½ cup water, salt and ground red pepper.

When lentils have cooked 10 minutes, stir in rice and seasoning packet. Cover tightly and simmer 5 minutes. Remove from heat. Stir in onion mixture and remaining 1 tablespoon oil; toss gently.

Makes 7 (1-cup) servings

Variation: For a more decorative dish, coat a 6-cup mold with cooking spray. Place rice mixture in mold and press down gently but firmly to allow rice mixture to stick together. Place a dinner plate on top of mold and invert mold onto plate. Tap gently on side and top of mold to release rice mixture and slowly remove mold. Garnish with red bell pepper strips.

Potatoes au Gratin

1 pound baking potatoes

4 teaspoons reduced-calorie margarine

4 teaspoons all-purpose flour

1 ¼ cups fat-free (skim) milk

¼ teaspoon ground nutmeg

¼ teaspoon paprika

Pinch ground white pepper

½ cup thinly sliced red onion, divided

⅓ cup whole wheat bread crumbs

1 tablespoon finely chopped red onion

1 tablespoon grated Parmesan cheese

1. Spray 4- or 6-cup casserole with nonstick cooking spray; set aside.

2. Place potatoes in large saucepan; add water to cover. Bring to a boil over high heat. Boil 12 minutes or until potatoes are tender. Drain; let potatoes stand 10 minutes or until cool enough to handle.

3. Melt margarine in small saucepan over medium heat. Add flour. Cook and stir 3 minutes or until small clumps form. Gradually whisk in milk. Cook 8 minutes or until sauce thickens, stirring constantly. Remove saucepan from heat. Stir in nutmeg, paprika and pepper.

4. Preheat oven to 350°F. Cut potatoes into thin slices. Arrange half of potato slices in prepared casserole. Sprinkle with half of onion slices. Repeat layers. Spoon sauce over potato mixture. Combine bread crumbs, finely chopped red onion and cheese in small bowl. Sprinkle mixture evenly over sauce.

5. Bake 20 minutes. Let stand 5 minutes before serving. Garnish as desired. *Makes 4 servings*

Potatoes au Gratin

Cheesy Broccoli

2 tablespoons CRISCO® Oil*

2 cups broccoli flowerets (bite-sized pieces)

3 tablespoons water

½ teaspoon salt

¼ cup freshly grated Parmesan cheese

*Use your favorite Crisco Oil product.

1. Heat Crisco Oil in wok or large skillet on medium-high heat. Add broccoli. Stir-fry 2 minutes.

2. Add water and salt. Cover pan. Steam 3 minutes. Remove broccoli from pan with slotted spoon. Toss with cheese. Serve immediately. *Makes 4 servings*

Prep Time: 5 minutes

Total Time: 10 minutes

Spinach, Bacon and Mushroom Salad

1 large bunch (12 ounces) fresh spinach leaves, washed, drained and torn

¾ cup sliced fresh mushrooms

4 slices bacon, cooked and crumbled

¾ cup croutons

4 hard-cooked eggs, finely chopped

Black pepper, to taste

¾ cup prepared HIDDEN VALLEY® Original Ranch® salad dressing

In medium salad bowl, combine spinach, mushrooms and bacon; toss. Top with croutons and eggs; season with pepper. Pour salad dressing over all. *Makes 6 servings*

a helping hand

GOOD EGGS: TO PRODUCE HARD-COOKED EGGS THAT AREN'T TOUGH AND RUBBERY, PLACE EGGS IN A SINGLE LAYER IN A SAUCEPAN AND COVER THEM WITH AT LEAST 1 INCH OF WATER. BRING THE EGGS TO A BOIL, REMOVE FROM HEAT AND LET STAND 15 TO 17 MINUTES BEFORE DRAINING AND COOLING.

Spinach, Bacon and Mushroom Salad

Herbed Asparagus

1 box (10 ounces)
BIRDS EYE® frozen
Asparagus Spears
or Asparagus Cuts

1½ tablespoons butter or
margarine, melted

2 teaspoons grated
Parmesan cheese

½ teaspoon dried basil

½ teaspoon dried
tarragon

- Cook asparagus according to package directions.
- Combine with remaining ingredients; mix well.
- Serve hot.   *Makes 3 to 4 servings*

Prep Time: 3 to 4 minutes

Cook Time: 5 to 6 minutes

Green Bean Almond Rice

1 tablespoon butter or
margarine

½ cup slivered almonds

½ cup chopped onion

⅓ cup chopped red bell
pepper

3 cups cooked brown
rice (cooked in beef
broth)

1 package (10 ounces)
frozen French-style
green beans, thawed

⅛ to ¼ teaspoon ground
white pepper

¼ teaspoon dried
tarragon leaves,
crushed

Melt butter in large skillet over medium-high heat. Add almonds; stir until lightly browned. Add onion and bell pepper; cook 2 minutes or until tender. Add rice, beans, white pepper and tarragon. Stir until thoroughly heated.   *Makes 8 servings*

Favorite recipe from USA Rice Federation

personal touch

EVEN ICE CUBES CAN BECOME DECORATIVE IF A LITTLE IMAGINATION IS APPLIED. FOR EXAMPLE, CUT LEMONS, LIMES OR ORANGES INTO TINY WEDGES AND DROP THEM INTO ICE CUBE TRAYS WHEN MAKING ICE FOR PUNCH, ICED TEA OR JUICE.

Green Bean Almond Rice

Mimosa Mold

1 ½ cups boiling water

1 package (8-serving size) *or* 2 packages (4-serving size) JELL-O® Brand Sparkling White Grape or Lemon Flavor Gelatin Dessert

2 cups cold seltzer *or* club soda

1 can (11 ounces) mandarin orange segments, drained

1 cup sliced strawberries

STIR boiling water into gelatin in large bowl at least 2 minutes or until completely dissolved. Refrigerate 15 minutes. Gently stir in cold club soda. Refrigerate about 30 minutes or until slightly thickened (consistency of unbeaten egg whites.) Gently stir for about 15 seconds. Stir in oranages and strawberries. Pour into 6-cup mold.

REFRIGERATE 4 hours or until firm. Unmold. Garnish as desired. Store leftover gelatin mold in refrigerator.   *Makes 12 servings*

Tip: To unmold, dip mold in warm water for about 15 seconds. Gently pull gelatin from around edges with moist fingers. Place moistened serving plate on top of mold. Invert mold and plate; holding mold and plate together, shake slightly to loosen. Gently remove mold and center gelatin on plate.

Prep Time: 15 minutes

Refrigeration Time: 4¾ hours

Pineapple Lime Mold

1 can (20 ounces) DOLE® Pineapple Chunks

2 packages (3 ounces each) lime gelatin

2 cups boiling water

1 cup sour cream

½ cup chopped walnuts

½ cup chopped DOLE® Celery

Drain pineapple, reserving syrup. Dissolve gelatin in boiling water. Add sour cream and reserved syrup. Chill until slightly thickened. Stir in pineapple, walnuts and celery. Pour into 7-cup mold. Chill until set.   *Makes 8 servings*

Mimosa Mold

Berry Cobbler

1 pint (2½ cups) fresh raspberries*

1 pint (2½ cups) fresh blueberries or strawberries,* sliced

2 tablespoons cornstarch

½ to ¾ cup sugar

1 cup all-purpose flour

1½ teaspoons baking powder

¼ teaspoon salt

⅓ cup milk

⅓ cup butter or margarine, melted

2 tablespoons thawed frozen apple juice concentrate

¼ teaspoon ground nutmeg

*One (16-ounce) bag frozen raspberries and one (16-ounce) bag frozen blueberries or strawberries may be substituted for fresh berries. Thaw berries, reserving juices. Increase cornstarch to 3 tablespoons.

1. Preheat oven to 375°F.

2. Combine berries and cornstarch in medium bowl; toss lightly to coat. Add sugar to taste; mix well. Spoon into 1½-quart or 8-inch square baking dish. Combine flour, baking powder and salt in medium bowl. Add milk, butter and juice concentrate; mix just until dry ingredients are moistened. Drop 6 heaping tablespoonfuls batter evenly over berries; sprinkle with nutmeg.

3. Bake 25 minutes or until topping is golden brown and fruit is bubbly. Cool on wire rack. Serve warm or at room temperature.

Makes 6 servings

a helping hand

COBBLERS ARE OFTEN CONFUSED WITH OTHER BAKED DESSERTS, SUCH AS CRUMBLES, CRISPS AND BUCKLES. THE COBBLER IS A BAKED, DEEP-DISH FRUIT DESSERT THAT IS TOPPED WITH A BISCUIT CRUST AND SPRINKLED WITH SUGAR. REGARDLESS OF NAME, THOUGH, THIS DESSERT IS A SUITABLE CHOICE FOR FALL AND WINTER PARTIES.

Berry Cobbler

Old-Fashioned Gingerbread

2 tablespoons margarine, melted and cooled

⅓ cup firmly packed brown sugar

¼ cup cholesterol-free egg substitute

¼ cup buttermilk

2 cups all-purpose flour

1½ teaspoons baking soda

1½ teaspoons ground ginger

1 teaspoon ground cinnamon

½ teaspoon salt

1 tablespoon instant decaffeinated coffee granules

1 cup hot water

½ cup molasses

¼ cup honey

1 jar (2½ ounces) puréed prunes

Reduced fat nondairy whipped topping (optional)

1. Preheat oven to 350°F. Spray 9-inch square or 11×7-inch baking pan with nonstick cooking spray; set aside.

2. Combine margarine, brown sugar, egg substitute and buttermilk in medium bowl; set aside. Combine flour, baking soda, ginger, cinnamon and salt in large bowl; set aside. Dissolve coffee granules in hot water in small bowl. Stir in molasses, honey and puréed prunes.

3. Add flour mixture alternately with coffee mixture to margarine mixture. Batter will be lumpy. *Do not overmix.*

4. Pour batter into prepared pan. Bake 40 to 45 minutes or until wooden pick inserted in center comes out clean. Cool in pan on wire rack. Before serving, top with whipped topping, if desired.

Makes 8 servings

personal touch

THE BEST HOLIDAY MEMORIES COME FROM TRADITIONS. THE ONLY RULES FOR GOOD TRADITIONS IS THAT THEY'RE REPEATED AND LOOKED FORWARD TO EACH YEAR. BE SENSITIVE TO GUESTS' REACTIONS TO HELP DETERMINE WHICH VARIABLES (SUCH AS MENU ITEMS OR ITINERARY) WILL BE A HIT YEAR AFTER YEAR.

Old-Fashioned Gingerbread

Orange-Almond Angel Food Cake

1 cup whole natural California Almonds

1 package (14.5 ounces) angel food cake mix, plus ingredients to prepare mix

1 ⅓ cups orange juice

2 tablespoons grated orange peel

Sorbet (optional)

Fresh fruit (optional)

Preheat oven to 350°F. Spread almonds in single layer on baking sheet. Toast in oven 12 to 15 minutes until lightly browned, stirring occasionally; cool and chop.

Prepare cake mix according to package directions, substituting orange juice for water called for in package directions. Fold in grated orange peel and ½ cup chopped almonds. Spoon batter into ungreased 10-inch tube pan. Sprinkle with remaining chopped almonds. Bake and cool according to package directions. Serve with sorbet and fresh fruit, if desired.   *Makes 10 servings*

Favorite recipe from Almond Board of California

Very Cherry Pie

4 cups frozen unsweetened tart cherries

1 cup dried tart cherries

1 cup sugar

2 tablespoons quick-cooking tapioca

½ teaspoon almond extract

Pastry for 2-crust, 9-inch pie

¼ teaspoon ground nutmeg

1 tablespoon butter

Combine frozen cherries, dried cherries, sugar, tapioca and almond extract in large bowl; mix well. (It is not necessary to thaw cherries before using.) Let stand 15 minutes.

Line 9-inch pie plate with pastry; fill with cherry mixture. Sprinkle with nutmeg. Dot with butter. Cover with top crust or cut top crust into strips for lattice top.

Bake in preheated 375°F oven about 1 hour or until crust is golden brown and filling is bubbly. If necessary, cover edge of crust with aluminum foil to prevent overbrowning.   *Makes 8 servings*

Note: 2 (16-ounce) cans unsweetened tart cherries, well drained, can be substituted for frozen tart cherries.

Favorite recipe from Cherry Marketing Institute, Inc.

Very Cherry Pie

Old-Fashioned Bread Pudding

2 cups fat-free (skim) milk

4 egg whites

3 tablespoons sugar

2 tablespoons margarine, melted

1 tablespoon vanilla

2 teaspoons ground cinnamon

12 slices whole wheat bread, cut into ½-inch cubes

½ cup raisins

½ cup chopped dried apples

1. Preheat oven to 350°F. Spray 2-quart casserole with nonstick cooking spray. Set aside. Combine milk, egg whites, sugar, margarine, vanilla and cinnamon in large bowl; mix well. Add bread, raisins and dried apples. Allow to stand 5 minutes.

2. Pour mixture into prepared casserole dish. Bake 35 minutes or until well browned. Cool in pan on wire rack.

Makes 12 servings

Classic Crisco® Single Crust

1⅓ cups all-purpose flour

½ teaspoon salt

½ cup Crisco® Shortening

3 tablespoons cold water

1. Spoon flour into measuring cup and level. Combine flour and salt in medium bowl. Cut in ½ cup shortening using pastry blender or 2 knives until all flour is blended to form pea-size chunks.

2. Sprinkle with water, 1 tablespoon at a time. Toss lightly with a fork until dough forms a ball.

3. Press dough between hands to form 5-inch "pancake." Flour rolling surface and rolling pin lightly. Roll dough into circle. Trim 1 inch larger than upside-down pie plate. Loosen dough carefully.

4. Fold dough into quarters. Unfold and press into pie plate. Fold edge under. Flute.

Old-Fashioned Bread Pudding

Boston Cream Pie

1 package DUNCAN HINES® Moist Deluxe® Yellow Cake Mix

4 containers (3½ ounces each) ready-to-eat vanilla pudding

1 container DUNCAN HINES® Creamy Homestyle Chocolate Frosting

1. Preheat oven to 350°F. Grease and flour two 8- or 9-inch round pans.

2. Prepare, bake and cool cake following package directions for basic recipe.

3. To assemble, place each cake layer on serving plate. Split layers in half horizontally. Spread contents of 2 containers of vanilla pudding on bottom layer of one cake. Place top layer on filling. Repeat for second cake layer. Remove lid and foil top of chocolate frosting container. Heat in microwave oven at HIGH (100% power) 25 to 30 seconds. Stir. (Mixture should be thin.) Spread half the chocolate glaze over top of each cake. Refrigerate until ready to serve. *Makes 12 to 16 servings*

Tip: For a richer flavor, substitute Duncan Hines® Butter Recipe Golden cake mix in place of Yellow cake mix.

Butter Almond Classic Cookies

1 cup (2 sticks) I CAN'T BELIEVE IT'S NOT BUTTER!® Spread

½ cup confectioners' sugar

½ teaspoon almond extract

1¾ cups all-purpose flour

½ cup finely chopped almonds

Additional confectioners' sugar

In large bowl with electric mixer beat I Can't Believe It's Not Butter! Spread and ½ cup sugar until light and fluffy, about 5 minutes. Beat in almond extract, then flour until blended. Beat in almonds. Turn dough onto plastic wrap and shape into flat circle. Cover and refrigerate at least 1 hour.

Preheat oven to 350°F. Divide dough into 8 pie-shaped wedges. On lightly floured surface, with lightly floured hands, roll each wedge into 1-inch-thick log. Cut each log in half forming 2 cookies, each about 2 to 3 inches long. Shape each cookie into crescent and arrange on *ungreased* baking sheets.

Bake 22 minutes or until very lightly golden. On wire rack, let stand 2 minutes; remove from sheets and cool completely. Before serving, sprinkle cookies with additional sugar.

Makes 16 cookies

Festive Mincemeat Tartlets

Pastry for double pie crust

1½ cups prepared mincemeat

½ cup chopped peeled, cored tart apple

⅓ cup golden raisins

⅓ cup chopped walnuts

3 tablespoons brandy or frozen apple juice concentrate, thawed

1 tablespoon grated lemon peel

Preheat oven to 400°F. Divide pastry in half. Refrigerate one half. Roll remaining half on lightly floured surface to form 13-inch circle. Cut six 4-inch rounds. Fit each pastry round into 2¾-inch muffin cup. Prick inside of crust with fork; set aside. Repeat with remaining pastry.

Bake unfilled pastry crusts 8 minutes. Meanwhile, combine mincemeat, apple, raisins, walnuts, brandy and lemon peel in medium bowl until well blended. Remove crusts from oven; fill each with rounded tablespoonful of mincemeat mixture. Press lightly into crust with back of spoon.

Bake 18 to 20 minutes more or until crust edges are golden. Cool in pan 5 minutes. Carefully remove from pan to wire rack. Serve warm or cool completely. *Makes 12 tartlets*

a helping hand

IN OLDEN DAYS, MINCEMEAT ACTUALLY CONTAINED MEAT, HENCE THE NAME. NOWADAYS, MINCEMEAT IS MADE OF MINCED FRUIT. HOWEVER, MINCEMEAT MAY CONTAIN BEEF LARD. IF ANY OF YOUR GUESTS ARE VEGETARIAN, CHECK LABELS CAREFULLY BEFORE PURCHASING.

Double Chocolate Treasure Cake

¾ **cup butter, softened**

1½ **cups sugar**

1 **egg**

1 **teaspoon vanilla**

2 **cups all-purpose flour**

⅔ **cup unsweetened cocoa powder**

2 **teaspoons baking soda**

¼ **teaspoon salt**

1 **cup buttermilk**

¾ **cup sour cream**

    Easy Chocolate Frosting (recipe follows)

    White Chocolate Drizzle (recipe follows)

Preheat oven to 350°F. Grease and flour 12-cup tube pan. Beat butter and sugar in large bowl with electric mixer at medium speed until light and fluffy. Beat in egg and vanilla until belnded. Combine flour, cocoa, baking soda and salt in medium bowl. Add flour mixture to butter mixture alternately with buttermilk and sour cream, beginning and ending with flour mixture. Beat well after each addition. Pour batter into prepared pan.

Bake 35 to 40 minutes or until cake begins to pull away from side of pan. Cool in pan 10 minutes. Remove from pan to wire rack; cool completely.

Prepare chocolate frosting; spread over cake. Prepare drizzle; drizzle over frosted cake. *Makes 12 to 16 servings*

Easy Chocolate Frosting: Beat ½ cup softened butter in large bowl with electric mixer at medium speed until creamy. Add 4 cups powdered sugar and ¾ cup cocoa altrnately with ½ cup milk; beat until smooth. Stir in 1½ teaspoons vanilla. Makes about 3 cups.

White Chocolate Drizzle: Combine ½ cup white chocolate chips and 2 teaspoons vegetable shortening in glass measuring cup. Heat in microwave on HIGH (100%) power 1 minute; stir. Continue heating at 15 second intervals, stirring, until smooth consistently. Makes about ½ cup.

Double Chocolate Treasure Cake

Classic Pumpkin Pie with Candied Pecan Topping

CRUST
- 1 (9-inch) Classic CRISCO® Single Crust (page 242)

FILLING
- 1 can (16 ounces) solid-pack pumpkin (not pumpkin pie filling)
- 1 can (12 ounces or 1½ cups) evaporated milk
- 2 eggs, lightly beaten
- ½ cup granulated sugar
- ¼ cup firmly packed light brown sugar
- 1 teaspoon cinnamon
- ½ teaspoon salt
- ½ teaspoon ginger
- ¼ teaspoon nutmeg
- ⅛ teaspoon cloves

TOPPING
- ¼ cup granulated sugar
- ¼ cup water
- 2 tablespoons butter or margarine
- 1 cup pecan pieces

1. Roll and press crust into 9-inch glass pie plate. Do not bake. Heat oven to 350°F.

2. For filling, combine pumpkin, evaporated milk, eggs, granulated sugar, brown sugar, cinnamon, salt, ginger, nutmeg and cloves in large bowl. Mix well. Pour into unbaked pie crust.

3. Bake at 350°F for 1 hour 10 minutes or until knife inserted in center comes out clean. *Do not overbake.* Cool completely.

4. Grease baking sheet lightly with shortening.

5. For topping, combine granulated sugar and water in small saucepan. Cook and stir on medium heat until sugar dissolves. Increase heat. Bring to a boil. Boil 7 to 8 minutes or until mixture becomes light golden brown, stirring frequently. Stir in butter and nuts. Stir briskly. Spread quickly in thin layer on baking sheet. Cool completely. Break into pieces. Sprinkle around edge of pie. (You might not use all of topping. Cover and store any extra for later use.) Refrigerate leftover pie.   *Makes 1 (9-inch) pie (8 servings)*

personal touch

SIMMERING PUMPKIN PIE SPICES OR VANILLA BEANS ON YOUR STOVE WITH PLENTY OF WATER CREATES JUST THE RIGHT ATMOSPHERE FOR A HOLIDAY PARTY. GUESTS WILL BE WELCOMED WITH A WARM AND INVITING AROMA THAT FILLS THE ENTIRE HOUSE.

Classic Pumpkin Pie with Candied Pecan Topping

fun with the family

menu ideas

HAUNTING DELIGHTS
Trick-or-Treat Punch (page 288)

Bat and Spook Pizzas (page 290)

Smucker's Spider Web Tartlets (page 286)

Frozen Witches' Heads (page 292)

Graveyard Pudding Dessert (page 292)

menu ideas

NUTCRACKER SWEETS
Hot Buttered Cider (page 316)

Party Cheese Wreath (page 304)

Holiday Candy Cane Twists (page 308)

Peanut Butter Reindeer (page 318)

Quick Candy Ornaments (page 314)

menu ideas

BIRTHDAY BASH
Cranberry-Orange Cooler (page 28)

BBQ Pork Sandwiches (page 150)

Melon Salad (page 188)

Merry-Go-Round Cake (page 256)

Ladybugs (page 254)

Watermelon Slices (page 258)

Ice Cream Cone Cakes

1 package DUNCAN HINES® Moist Deluxe® Cake Mix (any flavor)

1 container DUNCAN HINES® Creamy Homestyle Chocolate Frosting

1 container DUNCAN HINES® Creamy Homestyle Vanilla Frosting

Chocolate sprinkles

Assorted decors

Jelly beans

2 maraschino cherries, for garnish

1. Preheat oven to 350°F. Grease and flour one 8-inch round cake pan and one 8-inch square pan.

2. Prepare cake following package directions for basic recipe. Pour about 2 cups batter into round pan. Pour about 3 cups batter into square pan. Bake at 350°F 30 to 35 minutes or until toothpick inserted in center comes out clean. Cool following package directions.

3. To assemble, cut cooled cake and arrange as shown. Frost "cone" with Chocolate frosting, reserving ½ cup. Place writing tip in pastry bag. Fill with remaining ½ cup Chocolate frosting. Pipe waffle pattern onto "cones." Decorate with chocolate sprinkles. Spread Vanilla frosting on "ice cream" parts. Decorate with assorted decors and jelly beans. Top each with maraschino cherry.

12 to 16 servings

Tip: Use tip of knife to draw lines in frosting for waffle pattern as guide for piping chocolate frosting.

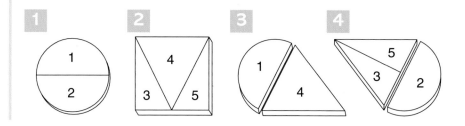

Ice Cream Cone Cakes

Ladybugs

¾ **cup shortening**

½ **cup sugar**

¼ **cup honey**

1 **egg**

½ **teaspoon vanilla**

2 **cups all-purpose flour**

⅓ **cup cornmeal**

1 **teaspoon baking powder**

½ **teaspoon salt**

DECORATIONS
   Orange and black icing and yellow candy-coated pieces

1. Beat shortening, sugar and honey in large bowl at medium speed with electric mixer until light and fluffy. Add egg and vanilla; mix until well blended.

2. Combine flour, cornmeal, baking powder and salt in medium bowl. Add to shortening mixture; mix at low speed until blended. Cover; refrigerate several hours or overnight, if desired.

3. Preheat oven to 375°F.

4. Divide dough into 24 equal sections. Shape each section into 2×1¼-inch oval-shaped ball. Place balls 2 inches apart on ungreased cookie sheets.

5. Bake 10 to 12 minutes or until lightly browned. Cool on cookie sheets 2 minutes. Remove to wire rack; cool completely.

6. Decorate cookies with icings and candies as shown in photo.

Makes 2 dozen cookies

personal touch

TURN THESE ADORABLE INSECTS LOOSE ON A PLATE OF GREEN TINTED COCONUT FOR A CONVINCING PRESENTATION.

Ladybugs

Merry-Go-Round Cake

1 package (6-serving size) JELL-O® Instant Pudding and Pie Filling, Vanilla Flavor

1 package (2-layer size) yellow cake mix

4 eggs

1 cup water

¼ cup vegetable oil

⅓ cup BAKER'S® Semi-Sweet Real Chocolate Chips, melted

⅔ cup cold milk

Sprinkles (optional)

Paper carousel roof (directions follow)

3 plastic straws

6 animal crackers

RESERVE ⅓ cup pudding mix. Combine cake mix, remaining pudding mix, eggs, water and oil in large bowl. Beat at low speed of electric mixer just to moisten, scraping sides of bowl often. Beat at medium speed 4 minutes. Pour ½ of the batter into greased and floured 10-inch fluted tube pan. Mix chocolate into remaining batter. Spoon over batter in pan; cut through with spatula in zigzag pattern to marbleize. Bake at 350°F for 50 minutes or until cake tester inserted in center comes out clean. Cool in pan 15 minutes. Remove from pan; finish cooling on rack.

BEAT reserved pudding mix and milk in small bowl until smooth. Spoon over top of cake to glaze. Garnish with sprinkles, if desired.

CUT 10- to 12-inch circle from colored paper; scallop edges, if desired. Make 1 slit to center (Diagram 1). Overlap cut edges to form carousel roof; secure with tape (Diagram 2). Cut straws in half; arrange on cake with animal crackers. Top with roof.

Makes 12 servings

Prep Time: 30 minutes

Baking Time: 50 minutes

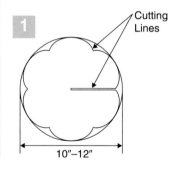

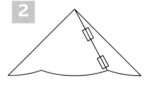

Merry-Go-Round Cake

Watermelon Slices

1 package DUNCAN
   HINES® Golden
   Sugar Cookie Mix

1 egg

¼ cup canola oil

1½ tablespoons water

12 drops red food
   coloring

5 drops green food
   coloring

Chocolate sprinkles

1. Combine cookie mix, egg, oil and water in large bowl. Stir until thoroughly blended; reserve ⅓ cup dough.

2. For red cookie dough, combine remaining dough with red food coloring. Stir until evenly tinted. On waxed paper, shape dough into 12-inch-long roll with one side flattened. Cover; refrigerate with flat side down until firm.

3. For green cookie dough, combine reserved ⅓ cup dough with green food coloring in small bowl. Stir until evenly tinted. Place between 2 layers of waxed paper. Roll dough into 12×4-inch rectangle. Refrigerate 15 minutes. Preheat oven to 375°F.

4. To assemble, remove green dough rectangle from refrigerator. Remove top layer of waxed paper. Trim edges along both 12-inch sides. Remove red dough log from refrigerator. Place red dough log, flattened side up, along center of green dough. Mold green dough up to edge of flattened side of red dough. Remove bottom layer of waxed paper. Trim excess green dough, if necessary.

5. Cut chilled roll, flat side down, into ¼-inch-thick slices with sharp knife. Place slices 2 inches apart on *ungreased* baking sheets. Sprinkle chocolate sprinkles on red dough for seeds. Bake at 375°F for 7 minutes or until set. Cool 1 minute on baking sheets. Remove to cooling racks. Cool completely. Store between layers of waxed paper in airtight container.

Makes 3 to 4 dozen cookies

personal touch

MAKE YOUR NEXT KIDS' PARTY A BEACH PARTY. BRING SPF 30 SUNSCREEN AS WELL AS PLENTY OF TREATS AND DRINKS TO KEEP EVERYONE SAFE AND SATIATED.

Beehives

1 tub (8 ounces) COOL
   WHIP® Whipped
   Topping, thawed

8 cupcakes

   Yellow jelly beans

   Chocolate decorating
      gel

   Black string licorice

SPOON whipped topping into large zipper-style storage bag. Close bag tightly, squeezing out excess air. Fold down top tightly; snip small piece (about ½ inch) off 1 corner.

HOLDING top of bag tightly, pipe whipped topping onto each cupcake to resemble beehives. Make stripes on jelly beans with decorating gel to resemble bumblebees; place on whipped topping. Add string licorice to form antennae. Serve immediately. Store leftover cupcakes in refrigerator. *Makes 8 servings*

Baseball Caps

1 cup butter, softened

7 ounces almond paste

¾ cup sugar

1 egg

1 teaspoon vanilla

¼ teaspoon salt

3 cups all-purpose flour

   Assorted colored
      icings and colored
      candies

1. Preheat oven to 350°F. Grease cookie sheets. Beat butter, almond paste, sugar, egg, vanilla and salt in large bowl at high speed of electric mixer until light and fluffy. Add flour all at once; stir just to combine.

2. Roll ¼ of dough on lightly floured surface to ⅛-inch thickness. Cut out 1-inch circles. Place cookies 2 inches apart on prepared cookie sheets.

3. Roll remaining dough into 1-inch balls.* Place one ball on top of half dough circle so about ½ inch of circle sticks out to form bill of baseball cap.

4. Bake 10 to 12 minutes or until lightly browned. If bills brown too quickly, cut small strips of foil and cover with shiny side of foil facing up. Let cool on baking sheet 2 minutes. Remove to wire rack; cool completely. Decorate with icings and candies.
Makes about 3 dozen cookies

Use a 1-tablespoon scoop to keep the baseball caps uniform in size and professional looking.

Peanut Butter and Jelly Sandwich Cookies

1 package (about 18 ounces) refrigerated sugar cookie dough

1 tablespoon unsweetened cocoa powder

All-purpose flour (optional)

1¾ cups creamy peanut butter

½ cup grape jam or jelly

a helping hand

FOR A DIFFERENT LOOK, CUT EACH SANDWICH COOKIE DIAGONALLY IN HALF. THIS CUTE PRESENTATION ALSO MAKES THEM A MORE MANAGEABLE SIZE FOR LITTLE TYKES.

1. Remove dough from wrapper according to package directions. Reserve ¾ section of dough; cover and refrigerate remaining ¼ section of dough. Combine reserved dough and cocoa in small bowl; refrigerate.

2. Shape reserved ¾ section dough into 5½-inch log. Sprinkle with flour to minimize sticking, if necessary. Remove chocolate dough from refrigerator; roll on sheet of waxed paper to 9½×6½-inch rectangle. Place dough log in center of rectangle.

3. Bring waxed paper edges and chocolate dough up and together over log. Press gently on top and sides of dough so entire log is wrapped in chocolate dough. Flatten log slightly on each side to form square. Wrap in waxed paper. Freeze 10 minutes.

4. Preheat oven to 350°F.

5. Remove waxed paper from dough. Cut dough into ¼-inch slices. Place slices 2 inches apart on ungreased cookie sheets. Reshape dough edges into square, if necessary. Press dough slightly to form indentation so dough resembles slice of bread.

6. Bake 8 to 11 minutes or until lightly browned. Remove from oven and straighten cookie edges with spatula. Cool 2 minutes on cookie sheets. Remove to wire racks; cool completely.

7. To make sandwich, spread about 1 tablespoon peanut butter on underside of 1 cookie. Spread about ½ tablespoon jam over peanut butter; top with second cookie, pressing gently. Repeat with remaining cookies. *Makes 11 sandwich cookies*

Peanut Butter and Jelly Sandwich Cookies

New Year's Chicken

1 whole chicken (about 3¾ pounds)

½ teaspoon salt

¼ teaspoon freshly ground black pepper

1 orange, peeled and separated into segments

1 medium onion, thinly sliced

½ cup kosher dry white wine

½ cup orange juice

2 tablespoons grated fresh ginger

2 tablespoons honey

Preheat oven to 350°F. Sprinkle chicken with salt and pepper. Place half of orange segments in chicken cavity. Pour onion slices in small shallow roasting pan or 8-inch square glass baking dish. Arrange remaining half of orange segments over onion slices in small shallow roasting pan. Pour wine over orange and onion slices. Place chicken, breast side down, over orange and onion mixture. Combine orange juice and ginger in glass measuring cup; pour over chicken. Bake, uncovered, 30 minutes.

Turn chicken, breast side up, and drizzle honey over surface. Bake 1 hour or until internal temperature of chicken reaches 180°F on meat thermometer inserted in thickest part of thigh. Baste with pan juices every 20 minutes. (If chicken is browning too quickly, tent with foil.) Transfer chicken to cutting board; tent with foil. Let stand 5 to 10 minutes.

Pour juices from roasting pan into small saucepan; discard orange and onion slices. Cook, stirring constantly, 2 to 3 minutes over medium-high heat or until slightly thickened. Serve with chicken.

Makes 6 servings

Favorite recipe from Hebrew National®

New Year's Chicken

Snowman Cupcakes

1 package (18.5 ounces)
    yellow or white cake
    mix, plus
    ingredients to
    prepare mix

2 (16-ounce) containers
    vanilla frosting

4 cups flaked coconut

15 large marshmallows

15 miniature chocolate
    covered peanut
    butter cups,
    unwrapped

Small red candies and
    pretzel sticks for
    decoration

Green and red
    decorating gel

Preheat oven to 350°F. Line 15 regular-size (2½-inch) muffin pan cups and 15 small (about 1-inch) muffin pan cups with paper muffin cup liners. Prepare cake mix according to package directions. Spoon batter into muffin cups.

Bake 10 to 15 minutes for small cupcakes and 15 to 20 minutes for large cupcakes or until cupcakes are golden and wooden toothpick inserted into centers comes out clean. Cool in pans on wire racks 10 minutes. Remove from pans to racks; cool completely. Remove paper liners.

For each snowman, frost bottom and side of 1 large cupcake; coat with coconut. Repeat with 1 small cupcake. Attach small cupcake to large cupcake with frosting to form snowman body. Attach marshmallow to small cupcake with frosting to form snowman head. Attach inverted peanut butter cup to marshmallow with frosting to form snowman hat. Use pretzels for arms and small red candies for buttons. Pipe faces with decorating gel. Repeat with remaining cupcakes.   *Makes 15 snowmen*

Spicy New Year's Wontons

1 tablespoon olive oil plus additional for greasing

2 green onions, finely chopped

½ pound ground turkey or chicken

½ cup drained canned black beans

½ cup salsa

32 to 34 wonton skins

1. Lightly brush baking sheet with small amount of oil; set aside.

2. Heat 1 tablespoon oil in medium skillet. Add green onions; cook and stir 1 minute. Add turkey; cook, stirring occasionally, 4 to 5 minutes or until turkey is no longer pink. Remove skillet from heat. Stir in beans and salsa.

3. With 1 point of wonton skin facing you, place about 1½ teaspoons turkey mixture on center of skin; moisten edges of skin with water. Fold wonton skin in half to enclose filling. Moisten points with water. Fold over wontons; press lightly to seal. Place on prepared baking sheet. Repeat with remaining turkey mixture and wonton skins.

4. Heat ¾ inch oil in wok or large skillet to 370°F. Fry wontons, a few at a time, 1 to 2 minutes or until golden brown. Remove from wok with slotted spoon; drain on paper towels. Serve warm with additional salsa. *Makes about 3 dozen wontons*

personal touch

PLAN AHEAD FOR YOUR NEW YEAR'S BASH. BE SURE TO TAKE THE TIME TO SEND OUT INVITATIONS EARLY. AROUND THE HOLIDAYS PEOPLE'S CALENDARS BOOK UP FAST, SO TO INSURE A GOOD TURNOUT, DON'T WAIT!

Guacamole Goal Post Dip

INGREDIENTS

1 can (16 ounces) refried beans

1½ cups salsa

1¾ cups (7 ounces) shredded Cheddar cheese, divided

2 containers (8 ounces each) guacamole

½ teaspoon ground cumin

⅓ cup finely chopped fresh cilantro or parsley

⅓ cup sour cream

6 pretzel rods

Whole pitted ripe olives

Pimiento strips (optional)

Tortilla chips

SUPPLIES

Pastry bag and small writing tip

Green ribbon or string

1. Spread beans onto bottom of 11×7-inch dish; top with salsa and 1½ cups cheese.

2. Combine guacamole and cumin in medium bowl. Spoon over cheese; carefully spread to cover. Sprinkle with cilantro.

3. Using pastry bag fitted with writing tip, pipe sour cream over cilantro to resemble yard lines of football field.

4. Using serrated knife, cut one 5½-inch piece from each of 4 pretzels. Use with remaining 2 pretzels to form goal posts, tying with ribbon to secure. Insert goal posts into dip.

5. Sprinkle remaining ¼ cup cheese in end zones. Stuff ½ of the olives with small strips of pimiento, if desired; place olives on dip to resemble football players. Serve with tortilla chips.

Makes 10 to 12 servings

a helping hand

KEEP IT SIMPLE! DON'T RUN YOURSELF RAGGED THE DAY OF THE PARTY. CHOOSE A FEW RECIPES YOU REALLY WANT TO MAKE AND THEN PROVIDE STORE-BOUGHT GOODIES LIKE CHIPS AND SALSA, MIXED NUTS, PRETZELS AND EVEN FRESH FRUIT. YOU TOO SHOULD ENJOY ALL THE GAME-DAY FESTIVITIES.

Guacamole Goal Post Dip

Football Salami Kick-Off

1 large loaf Italian bread*

HEBREW NATIONAL® Deli Mustard

1 tablespoon vegetable oil

⅔ cup chopped onion

⅓ cup chopped seeded red bell pepper

⅓ cup chopped seeded green bell pepper

1 (12-ounce) HEBREW NATIONAL® Beef Salami or Lean Beef Salami Chub, diced

8 eggs, beaten *or* 1½ cups cholesterol-free egg substitute

Salt

Freshly ground black pepper

Or, substitute 6 hoagie rolls for Italian bread loaf. Prepare and fill as directed for Italian bread loaf. Wrap each filled hoagie individually in aluminum foil; bake about 15 minutes or until heated through.

Preheat oven to 350°F. Slice bread in half lengthwise. Remove soft bread center; reserve for another use. Spread mustard evenly inside bread shells.

Heat oil in large nonstick skillet over medium heat. Add onion; cook 4 minutes. Add bell peppers; cook 4 minutes or until peppers are tender, stirring occasionally. Add salami; cook until heated through. Add eggs; increase heat to medium-high. Cook, stirring until eggs are set. Season with salt and pepper to taste.

Fill bread shells with salami mixture. Close sandwich; wrap tightly in aluminum foil. Bake 20 minutes or until heated through. Cut sandwich crosswise into 6 slices.   *Makes 6 servings*

a helping hand

WHEN SERVING WARM BEVERAGES AT YOUR SUPERBOWL PARTY, AN EASY WAY TO KEEP THEM WARM WITHOUT THE FUSS OF STANDING OVER THE STOVE IS TO PUT THEM IN A SLOW COOKER TURNED ON LOW. SIMPLY PLACE MUGS AND A LADLE NEAR THE SLOW COOKER SO GUESTS CAN HELP THEMSELVES THROUGHOUT THE DAY.

Football Salami Kick-Off

Conversation Heart Cereal Treats

2 tablespoons margarine or butter

20 large marshmallows

3 cups frosted oat cereal with marshmallow bits

12 large conversation hearts

1. Line 8- or 9-inch square pan with aluminum foil, leaving 2-inch overhangs on 2 sides. Generously grease or spray with nonstick cooking spray.

2. Melt margarine and marshmallows in medium saucepan over medium heat 3 minutes or until melted and smooth; stir constantly. Remove from heat.

3. Add cereal; stir until completely coated. Spread into prepared pan; press evenly onto bottom using greased rubber spatula. Press candies into top of treats while still warm, evenly spacing to allow 1 candy per bar. Let cool 10 minutes. Using foil overhangs as handles, remove treats from pan. Cut into 12 bars.

Makes 12 bars

Prep and Cook Time: **18 minutes**

a helping hand

FOR A WHIMSICAL TWIST ON THIS VALENTINE'S TREAT, USE A COOKIE CUTTER TO CUT OUT HEART SHAPES FOR ADDED FUN.

Conversation Heart Cereal Treats

Valentine Smoothie

1 cup vanilla low-fat yogurt

1 ripe banana, sliced

2 tablespoons strawberry jam

1 tablespoon honey or granulated sugar

3 or 4 drops red food coloring

1. Combine yogurt, banana, jam, honey and food coloring in blender container; cover. Blend on high 20 seconds or until foamy. Pour into 2 glasses; serve immediately. Garnish as desired.

Makes 2 servings

Cook's Notes: It's easy to change the flavors of this recipe to make it a year-round treat. Substitute your favorite flavor yogurt and use a fruit combination such as chopped seedless orange and sliced strawberries.

Prep and Cook Time: 3 minutes

Cupid Cakes

1 package (10 ounces) frozen strawberries, thawed

1 tablespoon powdered sugar

½ cup whipping cream, whipped

2 frozen all-butter pound cakes (10¾ ounces each), thawed

½ cup strawberry or seedless raspberry preserves

1. Drain strawberries, reserving 1 tablespoon juice. Discard remaining juice. Gently combine strawberries, reserved juice and powdered sugar with whipped cream; set aside.

2. Cut each cake into 12 slices. Spread 12 slices with about 1½ teaspoons preserves each. Top with remaining slices to make sandwiches, pressing gently to spread preserves to edges. Scrape excess preserves from edges. Place onto serving plates; top with whipped cream mixture.

Makes 12 servings

Prep and Cook Time: 15 minutes

Cupid Cake

Corned Beef and Cabbage with Parsley Dumplings

1 (4-pound) corned beef brisket, rinsed and trimmed

2 tablespoons TABASCO® brand Green Pepper Sauce

1 small green cabbage, coarsely shredded

PARSLEY DUMPLINGS

2 cups all-purpose flour

1 tablespoon baking powder

¼ teaspoon salt

1 cup milk

1 egg, beaten

2 tablespoons chopped fresh parsley

1 tablespoon butter or margarine, melted

2 teaspoons TABASCO® brand Green Pepper Sauce

Place corned beef in large saucepan with enough cold water to cover by 2 inches; add 2 tablespoons TABASCO® Sauce. Heat to boiling over high heat. Reduce heat to low; cover and simmer 2 hours, occasionally skimming surface.

During last 10 minutes of cooking corned beef, add cabbage to cooking liquid; return to boil over high heat. Reduce heat, cover and simmer 10 minutes or until cabbage is tender. Remove corned beef and cabbage to warm serving platter; keep warm. Reserve liquid in saucepan.

For Parsley Dumplings, combine flour, baking powder and salt in large bowl. Whisk milk, egg, parsley, butter and 2 teaspoons TABASCO® Sauce in small bowl until blended. Stir milk mixture into dry ingredients just until blended. Form dumplings by dropping tablespoonfuls of batter into reserved simmering liquid. Cover and simmer 10 minutes or until dumplings are cooked in center. Transfer dumplings to platter with corned beef and cabbage using slotted spoon.   *Makes 6 to 8 servings*

Corned Beef and Cabbage
with Parsley Dumplings

St. Patrick's Parfaits

2 cups cold milk

1 package (4-serving size) JELL-O® Pistachio Flavor Instant Pudding and Pie Filling

Chocolate sauce

2 cups thawed COOL WHIP® Whipped Topping

Chocolate shamrock cutouts (optional)

POUR milk into large bowl. Add pudding mix. Beat with wire whisk 1 to 2 minutes.

LAYER pudding, chocolate sauce and 1 cup of the whipped topping alternately in 4 parfait glasses. Garnish with remaining whipped topping and chocolate shamrock cutouts.

REFRIGERATE until ready to serve. *Makes 4 servings*

Hippity Hop Bunny Cake

2¼ cups BAKER'S® ANGEL FLAKE® Coconut

Red food coloring

2 baked 9-inch round cake layers, cooled

1 tub (8 ounces) COOL WHIP® Whipped Topping, thawed

Assorted candies

TINT ¼ cup of the coconut pink using red food coloring.

LEAVE 1 cake layer whole; cut remaining cake layer as shown in illustration. Using small amount of whipped topping to hold pieces together, arrange cake on serving tray as shown in photograph.

FROST cake with remaining whipped topping. Sprinkle center of bunny's ears with pink coconut. Sprinkle remaining 2 cups white coconut over bunny's head and outer edges of ears. Decorate with candies. Store cake in refrigerator. *Makes 12 to 16 servings*

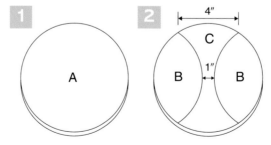

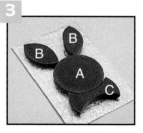

Hippity Hop Bunny Cake

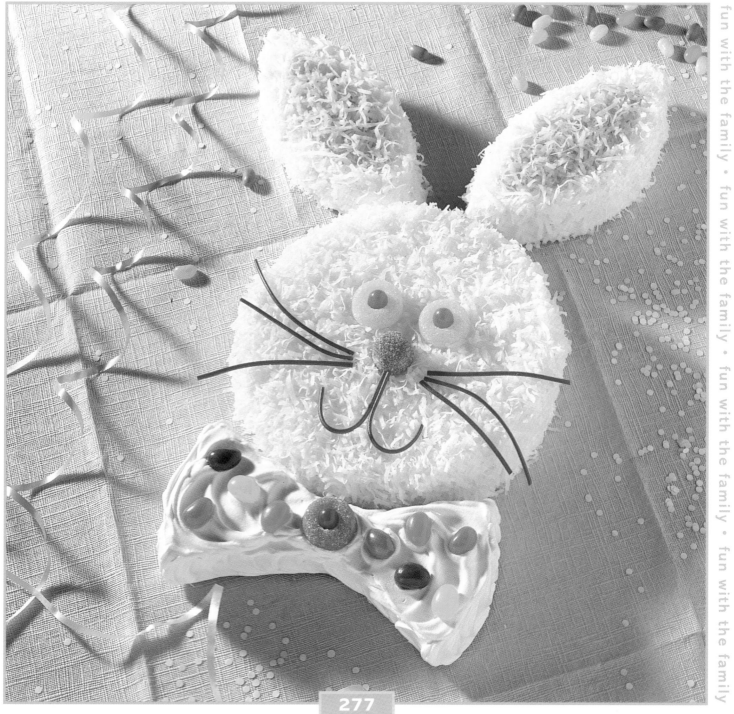

Bunny Pancakes with Strawberry Butter

Strawberry Butter (recipe follows)

2 eggs

2 cups buttermilk baking mix

1 cup milk

½ cup plain yogurt

Assorted candies

1. Prepare Strawberry Butter; set aside. Preheat electric skillet or griddle to 375°F.

2. Combine eggs, baking mix, milk and yogurt in medium bowl; mix well. Spoon scant ½ cup batter into skillet. With back of spoon, gently spread batter into 4-inch circle. Spoon about 2 tablespoons batter onto top edge of circle for head. Using back of spoon, spread batter from head to form bunny ears as shown in photo.

3. Cook until bubbles on surface begin to pop and top of pancake appears dry; turn pancake over. Cook until done, 1 to 2 minutes. Decorate with candies as shown in photo.

4. Repeat with remaining batter. Serve warm with Strawberry Butter.   *Makes about 12 (8-inch) pancakes*

Strawberry Butter

1 package (3 ounces) cream cheese, softened

½ cup butter, softened

⅓ cup powdered sugar

1½ cups fresh or thawed frozen strawberries

Place cream cheese and butter in food processor or blender; process until smooth. Add sugar; process until blended. Add strawberries; process until finely chopped.

Makes about 1⅓ cups

personal touch

TO HELP YOUR GUESTS KNOW HOW TO DRESS FOR YOUR GATHERING, SEND INVITATIONS THAT REFLECT THE MOOD OF THE PARTY. IF IT IS A MORE FORMAL AFFAIR, SEND INVITATIONS THAT HAVE AN ELEGANT FLAIR. IF CASUAL IS THE WAY TO GO, SEND INVITATIONS THAT ARE FUN AND COLORFUL.

Bunny Pancakes with Strawberry Butter

Easter Egg Cookies

1 package DUNCAN
   HINES® Golden
   Sugar Cookie Mix

¼ cup vegetable oil

2 egg whites

Assorted colored
   decors

Corn syrup

Food coloring

1. Preheat oven to 375°F.

2. Combine cookie mix, oil and egg whites in large bowl. Stir with wooden spoon until thoroughly blended.

3. Place 1 level measuring teaspoonful dough on ungreased baking sheet about 2 inches apart for each cookie. Flatten dough into egg shape (an oval with one narrow end and one wide end). Decorate half the eggs with assorted decors. Press lightly into cookie dough. Bake at 375°F for 6 to 7 minutes or until cookies are light golden brown around the edges. Cool 1 minute on baking sheets. Remove to cooling racks. Cool completely.

4. To decorate plain cookies, combine 1 tablespoon corn syrup and 1 or 2 drops food coloring in small bowl for each color. Stir to blend. Paint designs with tinted corn syrup using clean artist paint brushes. Sprinkle painted areas with colored decors, if desired. Store between layers of waxed paper in airtight container.

Makes 4 dozen cookies

Tip: Keep cookie dough an even thickness when shaping for more even baking.

personal touch

THE EASTER BUNNY CAME! PLACE THE EASTER EGG COOKIES IN A GRAPEVINE BASKET LINED WITH EASTER GRASS. SPRINKLE WITH JELLY BEANS AND MARSHMALLOW EGGS FOR EXTRA GOODIES FROM THE EASTER BUNNY.

Easter Egg Cookies

"Red, White and Blue" Mold

2¾ cups boiling water

1 package (4-serving size) JELL-O® Brand Strawberry Flavor Gelatin Dessert, or any red flavor

1 package (4-serving size) JELL-O® Brand Berry Blue Flavor Gelatin Dessert

1 cup cold water

1½ cups sliced strawberries

1 package (4-serving size) JELL-O® Brand Lemon Flavor Gelatin Dessert

1 pint (2 cups) vanilla ice cream, softened

1½ cups blueberries

STIR 1 cup of the boiling water into each of the red and blue gelatins in separate medium bowls at least 2 minutes until completely dissolved. Stir ½ cup of the cold water into each bowl.

PLACE bowl of red gelatin in larger bowl of ice and water. Stir until thickened, about 8 minutes. Stir in strawberries. Pour into 9×5-inch loaf pan. Refrigerate 7 minutes.

MEANWHILE, stir remaining ¾ cup boiling water into lemon gelatin in medium bowl at least 2 minutes until completely dissolved. Spoon in ice cream until melted and smooth. Spoon over red gelatin in pan. Refrigerate 7 minutes.

MEANWHILE, place bowl of blue gelatin in larger bowl of ice and water. Stir until thickened, about 7 minutes. Stir in blueberries. Spoon over lemon gelatin in pan.

REFRIGERATE 4 hours or until firm. Unmold. Garnish as desired.

Makes 12 servings

Prep Time: 45 minutes

Refrigeration Time: 4½ hours

"Red, White and Blue" Mold

fun with the family • fun with the family • fun with the family • fun with the family

fun with the family • fun with the family • fun with the family • fun with the family • fun with the family • fun with the family

Patriotic Parfaits

4 containers (3½ ounces each) tapioca pudding, chilled

8 vanilla sandwich cookies, crumbled

¾ cup fresh blueberries

½ cup strawberry ice cream topping, chilled

1. Place half of container of pudding into each of 4 (6- to 8-ounce) parfait glasses; top evenly with half of cookies. Sprinkle 2 tablespoons blueberries over each parfait. Repeat layer with remaining pudding and cookies.

2. Spoon 2 tablespoons strawberry topping and 1 tablespoon blueberries over cookies in each parfait.   *Makes 4 servings*

Serving Suggestion: Serve additional vanilla sandwich cookies with Patriotic Parfaits.

Cutting Corners: To crumble cookies quickly and neatly, place cookies in resealable plastic food storage bag. Crush with rolling pin or meat mallet.

Prep Time: 15 minutes

Firecrackers

5 cups BAKER'S® ANGEL FLAKE® Coconut

Blue food coloring

24 baked cupcakes, cooled

1 tub (12 ounces) COOL WHIP® Whipped Topping, thawed

Red decorating gel

Red string licorice

TINT coconut using blue food coloring.

TRIM any "lips" off top edges of cupcakes. Using small amount of whipped topping, attach bottoms of 2 cupcakes together. Repeat with remaining cupcakes. Stand attached cupcakes on 1 end on serving plate or tray.

FROST with remaining whipped topping. Press coconut onto sides.

DRAW a star on top of each firecracker with decorating gel. Insert pieces of licorice for fuses. Store cakes in refrigerator.

Makes 12 servings

Firecrackers

Smucker's® Spider Web Tartlets

INGREDIENTS:

1 (16-ounce) log
   refrigerated sugar
   cookie dough

Nonstick cooking
   spray or parchment
   paper

1 cup (12-ounce jar)
   SMUCKER'S® Apricot
   Preserves

¾ cup flour

1 tube black cake
   decorating gel

1. Preheat the oven to 375°F degrees. Unwrap cookie dough and place in medium mixing bowl. With floured hands, knead flour into cookie dough. Roll dough back into log shape, place on clean cutting board and cut into eight equal slices. With floured fingers, place dough circles onto baking sheet lined with parchment paper or sprayed with nonstick spray.

2. Gently press dough circles, flattening to make each one approximately 4 inches in diameter. With thumb and forefinger, pinch the edge of each dough circle to create a ridge all around. Pinch each dough circle along the ridge to make eight points.

3. Spread 2 tablespoons of Smucker's Jam (or Simply Fruit) onto each dough circle, making sure to spread it all the way to the edges and in the points. Refrigerate for 20 minutes. Bake 12 to 14 minutes or until edges are lightly browned.

4. Remove tartlets from baking sheet and cool on wire rack. When cool, use the black decorating gel to make a spider web design.

Makes 8 servings

personal touch

CREEPY AND SCARY IS THE THEME FOR THE NIGHT. USING ORANGE OR WHITE NAPKINS, PLACE A PLASTIC SPIDER RING AROUND THE NAPKIN AS A NAPKIN HOLDER. SET A NAPKIN AT EACH PERSON'S PLACE OR FILL A CALDRON WITH THEM IF YOU ARE HAVING A HALLOWEEN BUFFET.

Irresistible Peanut Butter Jack O'Lanterns

COOKIES

1¼ cups firmly packed
    light brown sugar

¾ cup creamy peanut
    butter

½ CRISCO® Stick or
    ½ cup CRISCO®
    all-vegetable
    shortening

3 tablespoons milk

1 tablespoon vanilla

1 egg

1¾ cups all-purpose flour

¾ teaspoon baking soda

¾ teaspoon salt

ICING

1 cup (6 ounces)
    semisweet chocolate
    chips

2 teaspoons Butter
    Flavor* CRISCO®
    Stick or 2 teaspoons
    Butter Flavor*
    CRISCO® all-
    vegetable
    shortening

*Butter Flavor Crisco is
artificially flavored.*

1. Heat oven to 375°F. Place sheets of foil on countertop for cooling cookies.

2. For cookies, place brown sugar, peanut butter; ½ cup shortening, milk and vanilla in large bowl. Beat at medium speed of electric mixer until well blended. Add egg; beat just until blended.

3. Combine flour, baking soda and salt. Add to shortening mixture; beat at low speed just until blended.

4. Pinch off pieces of dough the size of walnuts. Shape into balls. Place 3 inches apart on ungreased baking sheet. Flatten each ball with bottom of glass to approximately ⅜-inch thickness. Form into pumpkin shape, making indentation on top of round. Pinch off very small piece of dough and roll to form small stem. Attach to top of cookie. Score dough with vertical lines with small, sharp knife to resemble pumpkin.

5. Bake one baking sheet at a time at 375°F for 7 to 8 minutes or until cookies are set and just beginning to brown. *Do not overbake.* Cool on baking sheet 2 minutes. Remove cookies to foil to cool completely.

6. For icing, place chocolate chips and shortening in heavy resealable sandwich bag; seal bag. Microwave at 50% (MEDIUM) for 1 minute. Knead bag. If necessary, microwave at 50% for another 30 seconds at a time until mixture is smooth when bag is kneaded. Cut small tip off corner of bag. Pipe lines and faces on cookies to resemble jack o' lanterns.

Makes about 3 dozen cookies

Eyeballs

12 hard-cooked eggs

1 can (4½ ounces) deviled ham

⅓ cup mayonnaise

4 teaspoons prepared mustard

¼ cup drained sweet pickle relish

12 pimiento-stuffed olives, halved

1. Cut eggs lengthwise into halves. Remove yolks; place in small bowl. Mash egg yolks with fork; mix in deviled ham, mayonnaise, mustard and pickle relish. Season to taste with salt and pepper.

2. Spoon filling into egg halves. Garnish with olive halves to make "eyeballs."

3. To make extra scary bloodshot "eyeballs," spoon ketchup into small resealable plastic food storage bag. Cut off very tiny corner of bag; drizzle over eggs. *Makes 12 servings*

Cutting Corners: To save time, use leftover ketchup packets to drizzle over eggs to make bloodshot "eyeballs."

Prep Time: 25 minutes

Trick-or-Treat Punch

INGREDIENTS

Green food color

1 envelope (4 ounces) orange-flavored presweetened drink mix

1 can (12 ounces) frozen lemonade concentrate, thawed

1 bottle (2 liters) ginger ale

SUPPLIES

1 new plastic household glove

1. The day before serving, fill pitcher with 3 cups water; color with green food color. Pour into glove; tightly secure top of glove with twist tie. Cover baking sheet with paper towels; place glove on prepared baking sheet. Use inverted custard cup to elevate tied end of glove to prevent leaking. Freeze overnight.

2. When ready to serve, combine drink mix, lemonade concentrate and 4 cups water in large bowl; stir until drink mix is dissolved and mixture is well blended. Pour into punch bowl; add ginger ale.

3. Cut glove away from ice; float frozen hand in punch.
Makes 16 (6-ounce) servings and 1 ice hand

Variation: For an adult party, substitute 2 bottles (750 ml each) champagne for ginger ale, if desired.

Eyeballs

Bat & Spook Pizzas

4 (6-inch) Italian bread shells

⅔ cup pizza or spaghetti sauce

1 package (3½ ounces) pepperoni slices

4 slices (1 ounce each) mozzarella cheese

1. Preheat oven to 375°F. Place bread shells on ungreased baking sheet. Spread pizza sauce evenly onto bread shells; top evenly with pepperoni slices. Cut out ghost and bat shapes from cheese slices; place on pizza sauce. Bake 10 to 12 minutes or until cheese is melted. *Makes 4 servings*

Pumpkin Pizzas: Spread bread shells with pizza sauce as directed. Substitute process American cheese slices for mozzarella; cut into triangles. Place cheese triangles on pizza sauce to make jack-o'-lantern faces. Add ¼ cup broccoli florets for eyes and 2 cherry tomatoes, halved, for noses. Bake as directed.

Midnight Moon

1 round (8 ounces) Brie cheese

3 tablespoons plus 1½ teaspoons crumbled blue cheese

2 tablespoons plus 1½ teaspoons coarsely chopped walnuts

3 tablespoons apricot preserves, divided

Assorted crackers for serving

1. Preheat oven to 400°F. Cut Brie cheese horizontally into halves. Combine blue cheese and walnuts. Spread 4½ teaspoons apricot preserves on cut side of one half of Brie cheese; sprinkle with half of blue cheese-walnut mixture. Place remaining half of Brie cheese on top; spread with remaining 4½ teaspoons apricot preserves.

2. Wrap 3-inch-high strip of foil tightly around Brie; secure with piece of tape. Sprinkle remaining blue-cheese-walnut mixture over half of apricot preserves to form crescent moon shape.

3. Bake cheese in 8×8-inch baking pan 7 to 9 minutes or until soft and beginning to melt. Serve immediately with crackers. *Makes 8 servings*

Midnight Moon

Graveyard Pudding Dessert

3½ cups cold milk

2 packages (4-serving size) JELL-O® Chocolate Flavor Instant Pudding & Pie Filling

1 tub (12 ounces) COOL WHIP® Whipped Topping, thawed

1 package (16 ounces) chocolate sandwich cookies, crushed

Decorations: assorted rectangular-shaped sandwich cookies, decorator icings, candy corn and pumpkins

POUR milk into large bowl. Add pudding mixes. Beat with wire whisk or electric mixer on lowest speed 2 minutes or until blended. Gently stir in whipped topping and ½ of the crushed cookies. Spoon into 13×9-inch dish. Sprinkle with remaining crushed cookies.

REFRIGERATE 1 hour or until ready to serve. Decorate rectangular-shaped sandwich cookies with icings to make "tombstones." Stand tombstones on top of dessert with candies to resemble a graveyard. *Makes 15 servings*

Prep Time: 15 minutes

Refrigeration Time: 1 hour

Frozen Witches' Heads

3 whole graham crackers

6 scoops mint-flavored ice cream

6 chocolate-flavored ice cream cones

Red string licorice

Small round candies

Candy corn

1. Break graham crackers crosswise in half. Place 1 scoop ice cream on center of each cracker; top with inverted ice cream cone for hat.

2. Cut licorice into 1½-inch lengths; place next to cone for hair. Add candies for eyes and candy corn for noses. Freeze 4 to 6 hours or until firm. *Makes 6 servings*

Graveyard Pudding Dessert

Pumpkin Candy Brownies

1 package DUNCAN HINES® Chocolate Lovers Double Fudge Brownie Mix

2 eggs

⅓ cup water

¼ cup vegetable oil

1 cup DUNCAN HINES® Creamy Homestyle Chocolate Frosting

26 pumpkin candies

½ cup DUNCAN HINES® Creamy Homestyle Vanilla Frosting

Green food coloring

1. Preheat oven to 350°F. Line 26 (2-inch) muffin cups with foil liners or place on baking sheets.

2. Combine brownie mix, contents of fudge packet from mix, eggs, water and oil in large bowl. Stir with spoon until well blended, about 50 strokes. Fill each foil liner with 2 level measuring tablespoons batter. Bake 15 to 17 minutes or until firm. Cool 5 to 10 minutes in pans. Remove to cooling racks.

3. Place Chocolate Frosting in small saucepan. Melt on low heat, stirring constantly. Frost top of 1 warm brownie with generous ½ teaspoonful melted frosting. Top with 1 pumpkin candy; push down slightly. Repeat for remaining brownies. Cool completely.

4. Tint Vanilla Frosting with green food coloring. Place in decorating bag fitted with small leaf tip. Pipe 3 leaves around each pumpkin candy. Use small writing tip to pipe vines, if desired.

Makes 26 brownies

Cool Spiders

24 baked cupcakes, paper liners removed

1 tub (8 ounces) COOL WHIP® Whipped Topping, thawed

Chocolate sprinkles

Black licorice pieces and small candies for garnish

FROST tops and sides of cupcakes with whipped topping. Decorate with chocolate sprinkles. Insert licorice pieces into tops of cupcakes to create "spider legs." Top with candies for "eyes."

Makes 24 servings

Variation: To create "ladybugs," stir a few drops of red food coloring into whipped topping. Frost cupcakes as directed. Decorate with chocolate chips.

Prep Time: 5 minutes

Pumpkin Candy Brownies

Thanksgiving Grog

Thanksgiving Ice Ring (recipe follows)

1 can (12 ounces) frozen orange juice concentrate, thawed

2 quarts cranberry juice cocktail

1 quart apple cider

½ cup instant orange-flavored breakfast drink

¼ teaspoon red food color (optional)

1 bottle (1 liter) lemon-lime soda

1. The day before serving, prepare Thanksgiving Ice Ring; freeze until firm.

2. When ready to serve, combine all remaining ingredients except soda in large punch bowl; stir to blend well. Pour in soda.

3. Unmold ice ring; float in punch.

Makes 24 servings (about 5 ounces each)

Variation: For adult parties, stir in 1 cup vodka and ½ cup orange-flavored liqueur with the apple cider, if desired.

Thanksgiving Ice Ring

1 medium seedless orange, cut into wedges

½ to ¾ cup fresh or thawed frozen cranberries

3 cups apple cider

Arrange fruits on bottom of 3½-cup ring mold; fill with cider. Freeze until solid, about 8 hours or overnight. To unmold, dip bottom of mold briefly in hot water. *Makes 1 ice ring*

a helping hand

TURN YOUR THANKSGIVING ICE RING INTO SOMETHING SPECIAL. PLACE THE ORANGE SEGMENTS AND CRANBERRIES IN MUFFIN TINS, MEDELEINE PANS, MINI BUNDT PANS OR TART TINS. FILL WITH APPLE CIDER AND FREEZE.

Thanksgiving Grog

Fall Harvest Spice Cake

1 package
   (18.25 ounces)
   spice or carrot cake
   mix

1 cup water

3 eggs

⅓ cup vegetable oil

⅓ cup apple butter

   Maple Buttercream
   Frosting (recipe
   follows)

2 cups coarsely chopped
   walnuts

¼ cup semisweet
   chocolate chips,
   melted

¼ cup chopped almonds

2 tablespoons chopped
   dried apricots

2 tablespoons chopped
   dried cranberries*

2 tablespoons raisins

*If dried cranberries are
unavailable, use additional
chopped dried apricots and
raisins.

1. Preheat oven to 375°F. Grease and flour two 9-inch round baking pans.

2. Combine cake mix, water, eggs, oil and apple butter in medium bowl. Beat at low speed of electric mixer until blended; beat at medium speed 2 minutes. Pour batter into prepared pans.

3. Bake 35 to 40 minutes until wooden toothpick inserted into center comes out clean. Let cool in pans on wire rack 10 minutes. Remove to racks; cool completely.

4. Prepare Maple Buttercream Frosting.

5. Place 1 cake layer on serving plate; frost top with Maple Buttercream Frosting. Top with second cake layer; frost top and sides with frosting. Press walnuts onto side of cake.

6. Pipe chocolate onto cake for tree trunk. Combine almonds, apricots, cranberries and raisins. Sprinkle above and below trunk to make leaves.

Makes 12 servings

Maple Buttercream Frosting

4 tablespoons butter or margarine, softened

½ cup maple or pancake syrup

3 cups powdered sugar

In small bowl, beat butter and syrup until blended. Gradually beat in powdered sugar until smooth.

Fall Harvest Spice Cake

Cheese Pine Cones

2 cups (8 ounces) shredded Swiss cheese

½ cup butter or margarine, softened

3 tablespoons milk

2 tablespoons dry sherry or milk

⅛ teaspoon ground red pepper

1 cup finely chopped blanched almonds

¾ cup slivered blanched almonds

¾ cup sliced almonds

½ cup whole almonds

Fresh rosemary sprigs

Assorted crackers

Beat cheese, butter, milk, sherry and red pepper in medium bowl until smooth; stir in chopped almonds.

Divide mixture into 3 equal portions; shape each into tapered ovals to resemble pine cones. Insert slivered, sliced and whole almonds into cones. Cover; refrigerate 2 to 3 hours or until firm.

Arrange Cheese Pine Cones on wooden board or serving plate. Garnish tops with rosemary. Serve with assorted crackers.

Makes 12 to 16 appetizer servings

personal touch

FOR A SIMPLE YET SPECTACULAR CENTERPIECE ANY TIME OF YEAR, PICK YOUR FAVORITE GLASS BOWL AND FILL IT WITH WATER. PLACE FLOATING CANDLES IN THE BOWL WITH CRANBERRIES FOR WINTER, FRESH CUT FLOWERS FOR SUMMER AND GOURDS FOR FALL.

Candy Turkeys

1 ounce milk or
 semisweet chocolate
 confectionary
 coating

8 malted milk balls

8 chocolate candy stars

4 shortbread ring
 cookies

8 pieces candy corn

1. Melt chocolate coating according to package directions. Attach malted milk balls to candy stars with melted coating.

2. Cut each cookie in half. Using confectionary coating, attach 1 cookie piece to each malted milk ball for tail. With remaining confectionary coating, attach 1 candy corn to top of each malted milk ball for head.

Makes 8 turkeys

Crunchy Turkey Pita Pockets

1 cup diced cooked
 turkey or chicken
 breast or reduced-
 sodium deli turkey
 breast

½ cup packaged cole
 slaw mix

½ cup dried cranberries

¼ cup shredded carrots

2 tablespoons reduced-
 fat or fat-free
 mayonnaise

1 tablespoon honey
 mustard

2 whole wheat pita
 breads

1. Combine turkey, coleslaw mix, cranberries, carrots, mayonnaise and mustard in small bowl; mix well.

2. Cut pita breads in half; fill with turkey mixture.

Makes 2 servings

Dreidel Cake

1 package (2-layer size) cake mix, any flavor

1¼ cups water

3 eggs

¾ cup sliced or slivered almonds, toasted* and finely ground

¼ cup vegetable oil

½ teaspoon almond extract

1½ containers (16 ounces each) cream cheese frosting

Yellow and blue food colors

SUPPLIES
1 large tray or (15×10-inch) cake board, covered

Pastry bag and medium star tip

*To toast almonds, place in single layer on baking sheet. Bake at 350°F 7 to 10 minutes or until golden brown, stirring occasionally. Cool completely.

1. Preheat oven to 350°F. Grease and flour 13×9-inch baking pan. Combine cake mix, water, eggs, almonds, oil and extract in medium bowl. Beat at low speed of electric mixer until blended. Beat at medium speed 2 minutes. Pour batter into prepared pan.

2. Bake 35 to 40 minutes until wooden toothpick inserted into center comes out clean. Cool in pan on wire rack 10 minutes. Remove from pan; cool completely on rack.

3. If cake top is rounded, trim horizontally with long serrated knife. Cut cake as shown in diagram 1. Position cake pieces on tray as shown in diagram 2, connecting pieces with small amount of frosting. Frost center of cake with about ½ cup white frosting.

4. Tint about ¾ cup frosting yellow. To tint frosting, add small amount of desired food color; stir well. Slowly add more color until frosting is desired shade. Spread onto top and sides of cake.

5. Using diagram 3 as guide, cut out letter from waxed paper; position on cake as shown in photo. Trace around pattern with wooden toothpick; remove pattern. Tint remaining frosting blue. Spoon frosting into pastry bag fitted with star tip. Pipe stars to fill in symbol and pipe around top edge of cake as shown in photo.

Makes 12 servings

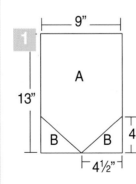

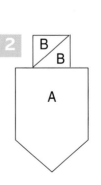

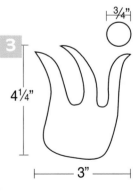

Dreidel Cake

Party Cheese Wreath

2 packages (8 ounces each) PHILADELPHIA® Cream Cheese, softened

1 package (8 ounces) KRAFT® Natural Shredded Sharp Cheddar Cheese

1 tablespoon chopped red bell pepper

1 tablespoon finely chopped onion

2 teaspoons Worcestershire sauce

1 teaspoon lemon juice

Dash ground red pepper

MIX cream cheese and Cheddar cheese with electric mixer on medium speed until well blended.

BLEND in remaining ingredients. Refrigerate several hours or overnight.

PLACE drinking glass in center of serving platter. Drop round tablespoonfuls of mixture around glass, just touching outer edge of glass to form ring; smooth with spatula. Remove glass. Garnish with chopped fresh parsley and chopped red pepper. Serve with crackers. *Makes 12 servings*

Variation: Substitute 2 packages (8 ounces each) PHILADELPHIA BRAND® Neufchâtel Cheese, ⅓ Less Fat than Cream Cheese for cream cheese.

Mini Cheeseballs: Shape cream cheese mixture into 1-inch balls. Roll in light rye bread crumbs or dark pumpernickel bread crumbs.

Prep Time: 15 minutes plus refrigerating

Queso Navidad

1 package (8 ounces) cream cheese, softened

1½ tablespoons diced green chiles

½ cup LAWRY'S® Chunky Taco Sauce

Crackers or chips

In small bowl, blend together cheese and chiles. Line a 1-cup mold or bowl with plastic wrap and pack cheese mixture into mold. Cover and refrigerate at least 1 hour. *Makes about 1 cup*

Presentation: Unmold onto serving platter, pour Chunky Taco Sauce over cheese mold and serve with crackers or chips.

Party Cheese Wreath

Christmas Carol Punch

2 medium red apples

2 quarts clear apple cider

½ cup SUN-MAID® Raisins

8 cinnamon sticks

2 teaspoons whole cloves

¼ cup lemon juice

Lemon slices

Orange slices

Core apples; slice into ½-inch rings. In Dutch oven, combine cider, apple rings, raisins, cinnamon and cloves. Bring to a boil over high heat; reduce heat to low and simmer 5 to 8 minutes or until apples are just tender. Remove cloves; add lemon juice, lemon and orange slices. Pour into punch bowl. Ladle into large mugs, including an apple ring, some raisins and citrus slices in each serving. Serve with spoons.   *Makes about 2 quarts*

Asparagus Wreath

1 pound fresh asparagus, ends trimmed

1 tablespoon butter or margarine

1 teaspoon lemon juice

6 thin slices pepperoni, finely chopped

¼ cup seasoned dry bread crumbs

Pimiento strips for garnish

1. Peel asparagus stalks, if desired. Steam asparagus in large covered saucepan 5 to 8 minutes or until crisp-tender.

2. Arrange asparagus in wreath shape on warm, round serving platter.

3. Heat butter and lemon juice in small saucepan until butter is melted; pour over asparagus. Combine chopped pepperoni and bread crumbs in small bowl; sprinkle over asparagus. Garnish, if desired.   *Makes 4 side-dish servings*

Asparagus Wreath

Holiday Candy Cane Twists

⅓ cup sugar

1 tablespoon ground cinnamon

1 can (11 ounces) refrigerated breadsticks

3 tablespoons butter or margarine, melted

Red tube icing (optional)

1. Preheat oven to 350°F. Spray baking sheet with nonstick cooking spray.

2. Combine sugar and cinnamon in small bowl; mix well.

3. Separate dough; roll and stretch each piece of dough into 16-inch rope. Fold rope in half; braid ends together and form into candy cane shape on prepared baking sheet.

4. Brush candy canes with butter; sprinkle with cinnamon-sugar.

5. Bake 12 to 15 minutes or until golden brown. Serve warm either plain or decorated with red icing as shown in photo.

Makes 8 servings

Christmas Tree Rolls: Make cinnamon-sugar with green colored sugar instead of granulated sugar. Stretch dough into 16-inch ropes as directed. Cut off ½ inch from 1 end of each rope for tree trunk. Shape ropes into tree shapes on prepared baking sheet; add trunks. Brush with butter and sprinkle with green cinnamon-sugar. Bake as directed. Decorate with red cinnamon candies.

a helping hand

THESE WARM, SWEET AND FESTIVE BREADSTICKS CAN BE PREPARED IN A SNAP AND ARE A PERFECT TREAT WHEN FRIENDS DROP IN FOR A VISIT. SERVE WITH SPICED CIDER, TEA, COFFEE OR HOT COCOA FOR A GREAT GOODY EVERYONE WILL ENJOY.

Holiday Candy Cane Twists

Mocha Nog

1 quart eggnog

1 tablespoon instant French vanilla or regular coffee granules

¼ cup coffee-flavored liqueur

1. Heat eggnog and coffee granules in large saucepan over medium heat until mixture is hot and coffee granules are dissolved; *do not boil.* Remove from heat; stir in coffee liqueur.

2. Pour eggnog into individual mugs.

Makes 8 servings

Prep and Cook Time: 10 minutes

Mini Mistletoe Turnovers

1 envelope LIPTON® RECIPE SECRETS® Onion Soup Mix

2 eggs, beaten

1 package (10 ounces) frozen chopped spinach, cooked and drained

2 cups (16 ounces) ricotta or creamed cottage cheese

1 scant cup (about 3 ounces) shredded mozzarella cheese

3 packages (8 ounces each) refrigerated crescent rolls

Preheat oven to 375°F.

In large bowl, combine onion soup mix, eggs, spinach and cheeses.

Separate crescent rolls according to package directions; cut each triangle in half (to make 2 smaller triangles) and flatten slightly. Place 1 tablespoon cheese mixture on center of each triangle; fold over and seal edges tightly with fork. Place on ungreased baking sheet; bake 15 minutes or until golden brown.

Makes 48 turnovers

Freezing/Reheating Directions: Tightly wrap turnovers in heavy-duty foil; freeze. To reheat, unwrap and bake as directed for 8 minutes or until heated through.

Mocha Nog

Star Christmas Tree Cookies

COOKIES

½ **cup vegetable shortening**

⅓ **cup butter or margarine, softened**

2 egg yolks

1 teaspoon vanilla extract

1 package DUNCAN HINES® Moist Deluxe Yellow or Devil's Food Cake Mix

1 tablespoon water

FROSTING

1 container (16 ounces) DUNCAN HINES® Creamy Homestyle Vanilla Frosting

Green food coloring

Red and green sugar crystals for garnish

Assorted colored candies and decors for garnish

Preheat oven to 375°F. For Cookies, combine shortening, butter, egg yolks and vanilla extract. Blend in cake mix gradually. Add 1 teaspoonful water at a time until dough is rolling consistency. Divide dough into 4 balls. Flatten one ball with hand; roll to ⅛-inch thickness on lightly floured surface. Cut with graduated star cookie cutters. Repeat using remaining dough. Bake large cookies together on *ungreased* baking sheet. Bake 6 to 8 minutes or until edges are light golden brown. Cool cookies 1 minute. Remove from baking sheet. Repeat with smaller cookies, testing for doneness at minimum baking time.

For Frosting, tint vanilla frosting with green food coloring. Frost cookies and stack beginning with largest cookies on bottom and ending with smallest cookies on top. Rotate cookies when stacking to alternate corners. Decorate as desired with colored sugar crystals and assorted colored candies and decors.

Makes 2 to 3 dozen cookies

Star Christmas Tree Cookies

Quick Candy Ornaments

1 package (7.5 ounces) hard candies, assorted colors

4 to 6 (2- or 3-inch) ovenproof open-topped cookie cutters

Clear nylon thread

1. Unwrap candies. Separate into colors; place each color in separate heavy resealable plastic food storage bag. Crush candies with rolling pin or hammer.

2. Cover baking sheet with foil; spray with nonstick cooking spray. Cut 6 pieces of foil, each about 8 inches square; fold each piece in half.

3. Place 1 cookie cutter in center of each piece of doubled foil; bring sides of foil up around cookie cutter, keeping foil in center as flat as possible. Press foil tightly to all sides of cutters. Place on prepared baking sheet, open tops facing up.

4. Preheat oven to 400°F. Spoon crushed candies into cookie cutters to a depth of about ½ inch. Bake 8 to 10 minutes or until candy is melted. Meanwhile, cut thread into 6 (8-inch) lengths; bring ends of thread together and tie in knots. Remove ornaments from oven. While candy is warm, soft and still in cutter, place knotted end of thread near top of each shape for hanging; press into ornament with handle of wooden spoon. Cool completely.

5. Peel foil off ornaments. Gently bend cutters to loosen ornaments. Break or scrape off ragged edges of ornaments with small knife.   *Makes 4 to 6 ornaments*

personal touch

THE PERFECT PARTY FAVOR: PURCHASE DIFFERENT SHAPED COOKIE CUTTERS TO MAKE THESE CANDY ORNAMENTS. ONCE BAKED, LEAVE THE COOKIE CUTTER AROUND THE CANDY AND WRAP IN COLORED PLASTIC WRAP. TIE WITH RIBBON AND PLACE IN A DECORATIVE BOWL FOR YOUR GUESTS TO TAKE AS THEY LEAVE.

Cranberry Chutney with Cream Cheese

INGREDIENTS
½ **cup granulated sugar**

¼ **cup packed brown sugar**

½ **cup water**

2 small tart green apples, peeled, cored and coarsely chopped

1 package (12 ounces) fresh cranberries

2 teaspoons grated orange rind

1 package (8 ounces) cream cheese

Green food color

Finely chopped nuts

Yellow bell pepper cutouts (optional)

Assorted crackers

SUPPLIES
Small pastry brush

1. Combine sugars and water in medium saucepan; bring to a boil. Stir in apples; simmer 3 minutes, stirring occasionally. Add cranberries and orange rind; cook 10 to 15 minutes or until cranberries are softened and chutney has thickened, stirring occasionally.

2. Spoon chutney into tightly covered container; refrigerate up to 2 weeks.

3. When ready to serve, cut block of cream cheese into Christmas tree shape, if desired; brush with food color to resemble branches of tree. Press nuts onto bottom of tree for "trunk." Remove a few cooked cranberries from chutney for garnish and use to decorate cream cheese tree along with bell pepper cutouts, if desired.

4. Serve chutney with cream cheese and crackers.

Makes 10 to 12 appetizer servings

Candy Cane Fudge

½ cup whipping cream

½ cup light corn syrup

3 cups semisweet chocolate chips

1 ½ cups powdered sugar, sifted

1 cup candy canes, crushed

1 ½ teaspoons vanilla

Line 8-inch baking pan with foil, extending edges over sides of pan.

Bring cream and corn syrup to a boil in 2-quart saucepan over medium heat. Boil 1 minute. Remove from heat. Stir in chocolate. Cook until chocolate is melted, stirring constantly. Stir in powdered sugar, candy canes and vanilla. Pour into prepared pan. Spread mixture into corners. Cover; refrigerate 2 hours or until firm.

Lift fudge out of pan using foil; remove foil. Cut into 1-inch squares. Store in airtight container.

Makes about 2 pounds or 64 pieces

Hot Buttered Cider

⅓ cup packed brown sugar

¼ cup butter or margarine, softened

¼ cup honey

¼ teaspoon ground cinnamon

¼ teaspoon ground nutmeg

Apple cider or juice

1. Beat sugar, butter, honey, cinnamon and nutmeg until well blended and fluffy. Place butter mixture in tightly covered container. Refrigerate up to 2 weeks. Bring butter mixture to room temperature before using.

2. To serve, heat apple cider in large saucepan over medium heat until hot. Fill individual mugs with hot apple cider; stir in 1 tablespoon batter per 1 cup apple cider.   *Makes 12 servings*

Prep and Cook Time: 15 minutes

Candy Cane Fudge

Peanut Butter Reindeer

COOKIES

1 package DUNCAN HINES® Peanut Butter Cookie Mix

1 egg

¼ cup vegetable oil

4 teaspoons all-purpose flour

ASSORTED DECORATIONS

Miniature semisweet chocolate chips

Vanilla milk chips

Candy-coated semisweet chocolate chips

Colored sprinkles

1. For Cookies, combine cookie mix, peanut butter packet from mix, egg and oil in large bowl. Stir until thoroughly blended. Form dough into ball; divide in half. Place 2 teaspoons flour in gallon size (10⁹⁄₁₆×11-inch) resealable plastic bag. Place dough in center of bag (do not seal). Roll dough with rolling pin out to edges of bag. Slide bag onto baking sheet. Repeat with remaining 2 teaspoons flour, second plastic bag and remaining dough ball. Chill in refrigerator at least 1 hour.

2. Preheat oven to 375°F.

3. Use scissors to cut one bag down center and across ends. Turn plastic back to uncover dough. Cut reindeer shapes, dipping cookie cutter in flour after each cut. Transfer cutout cookies using floured pancake turner to ungreased baking sheets. Decorate as desired making eyes, mouth, nose and tail with assorted decorations. Bake at 375°F for 5 to 7 minutes or until set but not browned. Cool 2 minutes on baking sheets. Remove to cooling racks. Cool completely. Repeat with remaining chilled dough. Store cookies between layers of waxed paper in airtight container.

Makes about 4 dozen cookies

Tips: Reroll dough by folding plastic back over dough. To use as ornaments, press end of drinking straw in top of each unbaked cookie to make hole. Press straw through cookies again after baking. String ribbon through holes of cooled cookies. Tie at top.

Peanut Butter Reindeer

the
perfect end

menu ideas

BAKE-SALE FAVORITES
Orange Cinnamon Swirl Bread (page 52)

Oreo® Brownie Treats (page 332)

Colorful S'mores Squares (page 331)

Luscious Key Lime Cake (page 346)

Old-Fashioned Creamy Fudge
(page 371)

menu ideas

CHOCOHOLICS' DREAM
Double Chocolate Chunk Cookies
(page 328)

Chocolate Hazelnut Pie (page 358)

Chocolate Raspberry Torte (page 344)

Cappuccino Bon Bons (page 362)

menu ideas

AFTERNOON TEA
Walnut Crescents (page 331)

Hazelnut Biscotti (page 326)

Honey-Pecan Coffee Cake (page 64)

Marbled Pumpkin Cheesecake Squares (page 330)

Argentinean Caramel-Filled Crescents (Pasteles)

3 cups all-purpose flour

½ cup powdered sugar

1 teaspoon baking powder

¼ teaspoon salt

1 cup butter, cut into small pieces

6 to 7 tablespoons ice water

½ package (14 ounces) caramel candies, unwrapped

2 tablespoons milk

½ cup flaked coconut

1 large egg

1 tablespoon water

Place flour, powdered sugar, baking powder and salt in large bowl; stir to combine. Cut butter into flour mixture with pastry blender or 2 knives until mixture forms pea-sized pieces. Add water, 1 tablespoon at a time; toss with fork until mixture holds together. Divide dough in half; cover and refrigerate 30 minutes or until firm.

Meanwhile, melt caramels and milk in medium saucepan over low heat, stirring constantly; stir in coconut with spoon. Remove from heat; cool.

Working with 1 portion at a time, roll out dough on lightly floured surface to ⅛-inch thickness. Cut dough with 3-inch round cookie cutter. Reroll trimmings and cut out more cookies.

Preheat oven to 400°F. Grease cookie sheets; set aside. Beat egg and water in cup. Place ½ teaspoon caramel mixture in center of each dough round. Moisten edge of dough round with egg mixture. Fold dough in half; press edges firmly to seal in filling. Press edge with fork. Place cookies on prepared cookie sheets; brush with egg mixture. Cut 3 slashes across top of each cookie with tip of utility knife. Bake 15 to 20 minutes or until golden brown. Remove cookies to wire racks; cool completely. Store tightly covered at room temperature.

Note: These cookies do not freeze well.

Makes about 4 dozen cookies

Argentinean Caramel-Filled Crescents (Pasteles)

Double Chocolate Oat Cookies

1 package (12 ounces)
  semi-sweet
  chocolate pieces,
  divided (about
  2 cups)

½ cup margarine or
  butter, softened

½ cup sugar

1 egg

¼ teaspoon vanilla

¾ cup all-purpose flour

¾ cup QUAKER® Oats
  (quick or old
  fashioned,
  uncooked)

1 teaspoon baking
  powder

¼ teaspoon baking soda

¼ teaspoon salt
  (optional)

Preheat oven to 375°F. Melt 1 cup chocolate pieces in small saucepan; set aside. Beat margarine and sugar until fluffy; add melted chocolate, egg and vanilla. Add combined flour, oats, baking powder, baking soda and salt; mix well. Stir in remaining chocolate pieces. Drop by rounded tablespoonfuls onto ungreased cookie sheet. Bake 8 to 10 minutes. Cool 1 minute on cookie sheet; remove to wire rack.   *Makes about 3 dozen cookies*

a helping hand

BAKE COOKIES ON THE MIDDLE RACK OF THE OVEN, ONE PAN AT A TIME. UNEVEN BROWNING CAN OCCUR IF BAKING ON MORE THAN ONE RACK AT THE SAME TIME.

Double Chocolate Oat Cookies

Hazelnut Biscotti

6 raw hazelnuts

2 tablespoons margarine

¼ cup sugar

2 egg whites, lightly beaten

1½ teaspoons vanilla

1½ cups all-purpose flour

½ teaspoon baking powder

⅛ teaspoon salt

½ teaspoon grated orange peel

1. Preheat oven to 375°F. Place hazelnuts in shallow baking pan; toast 7 to 8 minutes or until rich golden brown. Set aside. *Reduce oven temperature to 325°F.* Spray cookie sheet with nonstick cooking spray; set aside.

2. Combine margarine and sugar in medium bowl; mix well. Add egg whites and vanilla; mix well. Combine flour, baking powder, salt and orange peel in large bowl; mix well. Finely chop toasted hazelnuts; stir into flour mixture. Add egg white mixture to flour mixture; blend well.

3. Divide dough in half. Shape half of dough into log on lightly floured surface. (Dough will be fairly soft.) Repeat with remaining half of dough to form second log. Bake both logs 25 minutes or until wooden pick inserted in center of logs comes out clean. Cool on wire rack. *Reduce oven temperature to 300°F.*

4. When cool enough to handle, cut each log into 8 (½-inch) slices. Bake slices 12 minutes. Turn slices over; bake additional 12 minutes or until golden brown on both sides.

Makes 16 servings

Buttery Black Raspberry Bars

1 cup butter or margarine

1 cup sugar

2 egg yolks

2 cups all-purpose flour

1 cup chopped walnuts

½ cup SMUCKER'S® Seedless Black Raspberry Jam

Beat butter until soft and creamy. Gradually add sugar, beating until mixture is light and fluffy. Add egg yolks; blend well. Gradually add flour; mix thoroughly. Fold in walnuts.

Spoon half of batter into greased 8-inch square pan; spread evenly. Top with jam; cover with remaining batter.

Bake at 325°F for 1 hour or until lightly browned. Cool and cut into 2×1-inch bars.

Makes 32 bars

Hazelnut Biscotti

Baker's® Double Chocolate Chunk Cookies

1 pacakge (8 squares)
BAKER'S® Semi-
Sweet Chocolate,
divided

½ cup (1 stick) butter *or*
margarine

½ cup granulated sugar

¼ cup firmly packed
brown sugar

1 egg

1 teaspoon vanilla

1 cup flour

½ teaspoon CALUMET®
Baking Powder

¼ teaspoon salt

¾ cup chopped walnuts
(optional)

HEAT oven to 375°F.

MICROWAVE 1 square chocolate in microwaveable bowl on HIGH 1 to 2 minutes until almost melted, stirring halfway through heating time. Stir until chocolate is completely melted.

CUT 3 squares chocolate into large (½-inch) chunks; set aside.

BEAT butter until light and fluffy. Gradually beat in sugars. Mix in egg and vanilla. Stir in melted chocolate. Mix in flour, baking powder and salt. Stir in chocolate chunks and walnuts. Refrigerate dough 30 minutes.

DROP dough by rounded tablespoonfuls, about 2 inches apart, onto greased cookie sheets.

BAKE for 8 to 10 minutes or until lightly browned. Cool 2 minutes; remove from cookie sheets.

MICROWAVE remaining 4 squares chocolate in microwaveable bowl on HIGH 1½ to 2 minutes until almost melted, stirring halfway through heating time. Stir until completely melted.

DIP ½ of each cookie into melted chocolate. Let stand until chocolate is firm.   *Makes about 2 dozen (3-inch) cookies*

Note: Recipe can be doubled, tripled or even quadrupled.

Alternate Method: Heat chocolate in heavy saucepan on very low heat; stirring constantly, until just melted. Remove from heat. Continue as directed above.

Tip: Do not overbake cookies. They will be soft when done and firm up upon cooling.

Baker's® Double Chocolate Chunk Cookies

Marbled Pumpkin Cheesecake Squares

¼ **cup reduced-fat cream cheese, softened**

2 **tablespoons granulated sugar**

3 **tablespoons egg substitute**

1 **cup packed brown sugar**

½ **cup Prune Purée (recipe follows) or prepared prune butter**

2 **egg whites**

1½ **teaspoons vanilla**

1 **cup all-purpose flour**

1 **teaspoon baking powder**

¾ **teaspoon ground cinnamon**

¼ **teaspoon ground ginger**

¼ **teaspoon salt**

⅛ **teaspoon ground cloves**

¾ **cup canned pumpkin**

Preheat oven to 350°F. Coat 8-inch square baking dish or pan with vegetable cooking spray. In small bowl, beat cream cheese and granulated sugar until blended. Gradually add egg substitute, beating until blended. Set aside. In large bowl, beat brown sugar, Prune Purée, egg whites and vanilla until well blended. In medium bowl, combine flour, baking powder, cinnamon, ginger, salt and cloves; stir into brown sugar mixture until well blended. Beat in pumpkin. Spread batter evenly in prepared baking dish. Drop heaping tablespoonfuls of cream cheese mixture over batter. Using knife, gently swirl cream cheese mixture into batter. Bake in center of oven 25 to 30 minutes or until pick inserted into center comes out clean. Cool in baking dish 15 minutes. Cut into squares. Serve warm with fat-free vanilla ice cream or frozen yogurt, if desired. *Makes 9 servings*

Prune Purée: Combine 1⅓ cups (8 ounces) pitted prunes and 6 tablespoons hot water in container of food processor or blender. Pulse on and off until prunes are finely chopped and smooth. Store leftovers in a covered container in the refrigerator for up to two months. Makes 1 cup.

Favorite recipe from California Prune Board

Walnut Crescents

3¾ cups flour

½ teaspoon cinnamon

1½ cups (3 sticks) MAZOLA® Margarine or butter

¾ cup KARO® Light or Dark Corn Syrup

1 tablespoon vanilla

2¼ cups ground walnuts

1½ cups confectioners' sugar

1. In medium bowl combine flour and cinnamon; set aside.

2. In large bowl with mixer at medium speed, beat margarine until creamy. Gradually beat in corn syrup and vanilla until well blended. Stir in flour mixture and walnuts.

3. Cover; refrigerate several hours or until easy to handle.

4. Preheat oven to 350°F. Shape rounded teaspoonfuls of dough into 2-inch-long rolls. Place 2 inches apart on ungreased cookie sheets, curving to form crescents.

5. Bake 15 to 18 minutes or until bottoms are lightly browned. Remove from cookie sheets; cool completely on wire racks. Roll in confectioners' sugar. *Makes about 8 dozen cookies*

Prep Time: 30 minutes, plus chilling

Bake Time: 15 to 18 minutes, plus cooling

Colorful S'mores Squares

½ cup (1 stick) butter or margarine, softened

1 cup granulated sugar

3 large eggs

1 teaspoon vanilla extract

2 cups graham cracker crumbs

1¾ cups "M&M's"® Chocolate Mini Baking Bits, divided

1 cup marshmallow creme

Preheat oven to 350°F. Lightly grease 13×9×2-inch pan. In large bowl cream butter and sugar until light and fluffy; beat in eggs and vanilla. Stir in graham cracker crumbs until well blended. Stir in *1 cup "M&M's"® Chocolate Mini Baking Bits.* Spread batter into prepared pan; bake 30 minutes. Dollop marshmallow creme over hot crust; spread gently and evenly over crust. Sprinkle with remaining ¾ *cup "M&M's"® Chocolate Mini Baking Bits;* bake 5 minutes. Cool completely. Cut into squares. *Makes 24 squares*

Oreo® Brownie Treats

15 OREO® Chocolate Sandwich Cookies, coarsely chopped

1 (21½-ounce) package deluxe fudge brownie mix, batter prepared according to package directions

2 pints ice cream, any flavor

Stir cookie pieces into prepared brownie batter. Grease 13×9-inch baking pan; pour batter into pan. Bake according to brownie mix package directions for time and temperature. Cool. To serve, cut into 12 squares and top each with a scoop of ice cream.

Makes 12 servings

Pecan Date Bars

CRUST
1 package DUNCAN HINES® Moist Deluxe White Cake Mix

⅓ cup shortening plus additional for greasing

1 egg

TOPPING
1¼ cups chopped pecans

1 (8-ounce) package chopped dates

1 cup water

½ teaspoon vanilla extract

Confectioners' sugar

1. Preheat oven to 350°F. Grease and flour 13×9-inch baking pan.

2. For crust, cut ⅓ cup shortening into cake mix with pastry blender or 2 knives until mixture resembles coarse crumbs. Add egg; stir well (mixture will be crumbly). Press mixture into bottom of prepared pan.

3. For topping, combine pecans, dates and water in medium saucepan. Bring to a boil. Reduce heat; simmer until mixture thickens, stirring constantly. Remove from heat. Stir in vanilla extract. Spread date mixture evenly over crust. Bake 25 to 30 minutes. Cool completely. Dust with confectioners' sugar.

Makes about 32 bars

Pecan Date Bars

Turtle Cheesecake

6 tablespoons reduced-calorie margarine

1½ cups graham cracker crumbs

2 envelopes unflavored gelatin

2 containers (8 ounces each) fat-free cream cheese

2 cups 1% low-fat cottage cheese

1 cup sugar

1½ teaspoons vanilla

1 container (8 ounces) reduced-fat nondairy whipped topping, thawed

¼ cup prepared fat-free caramel topping

¼ cup prepared fat-free hot fudge topping

¼ cup chopped pecans

1. Spray bottom and side of 9-inch springform pan with nonstick cooking spray. Preheat oven to 350°F. Melt margarine in small saucepan over medium heat. Stir in graham cracker crumbs. Press crumb mixture firmly onto side or bottom of prepared pan. Bake 10 minutes; cool.

2. Place ½ cup cold water in small saucepan; sprinkle gelatin over water. Let stand 3 minutes to soften. Heat gelatin mixture over low heat until completely dissolved, stirring constantly.

3. Combine cream cheese, cottage cheese, sugar and vanilla in food processor or blender; process until smooth. Add gelatin mixture; process until well blended. Fold in whipped topping. Pour into prepared crust. Refrigerate 4 hours or until set.

4. Loosen cake from rim of pan. Remove side of pan from cake. Drizzle caramel and hot fudge toppings over cheesecake. Sprinkle pecans evenly over top of cake before serving.

Makes 16 servings

personal touch

SAVOR YOUR DESSERT LATER. WHY RUSH INTO A SPECTACULAR DESSERT RIGHT AFTER A FABULOUS MEAL WHEN EVERYONE IS STILL STUFFED FROM DINNER. RETIRE TO THE LIVING ROOM AND RELAX BY A FIRE. DESSERT AND COFFEE CAN BE SERVED THERE LATER WHILE EVERYONE IS RELAXING AND ENJOYING EACH OTHER'S COMPANY.

Turtle Cheesecake

Chocolate Almond Confection Cake

CAKE

1 package (7 ounces) pure almond paste

½ cup vegetable oil, divided plus additional for greasing

3 eggs

1 package DUNCAN HINES® Moist Deluxe Devil's Food Cake Mix

1⅓ cups water

GLAZE

1 package (6 ounces) semisweet chocolate chips

3 tablespoons cherry jelly or seedless red raspberry jam

2 tablespoons butter or margarine

1 tablespoon light corn syrup

Natural sliced almonds, for garnish

Candied whole maraschino cherries or fresh raspberries, for garnish

1. Preheat oven to 350°F. Grease and flour 10-inch Bundt® or tube pan.

2. For cake, combine almond paste and 2 tablespoons oil in large bowl. Beat at medium speed with electric mixer until blended. Add remaining oil, 2 tablespoons at a time, until blended. Add 1 egg; beat at medium speed until blended. Add remaining 2 eggs; beat until smooth. Add cake mix and water; beat at medium speed for 2 minutes. Pour into pan. Bake at 350°F for 50 to 55 minutes or until toothpick inserted in center comes out clean. Cool in pan 25 minutes. Invert onto cooling rack. Cool completely.

3. For glaze, place chocolate chips, cherry jelly, butter and corn syrup in microwave-safe medium bowl. Microwave at HIGH (100% power) for 1 to 1½ minutes. Stir until melted and smooth. Glaze top of cake. Garnish with sliced almonds and candied maraschino cherries. *Makes 12 to 16 servings*

Tip: This recipe may also be prepared in the food processor. Place almond paste in work bowl with knife blade. Process until finely chopped. Add cake mix, eggs, water and oil. Process for 1 minute or until smooth. Bake and cool as directed above.

Chocolate Almond Confection Cake

Fig and Hazelnut Cake

¾ cup hazelnuts or filberts (about 4 ounces), skins removed and coarsely chopped

¾ cup whole dried figs (about 4 ounces), coarsely chopped

⅔ cup slivered blanched almonds (about 3 ounces), coarsely chopped

⅓ cup diced candied orange peel

⅓ cup diced candied lemon peel

3 ounces semisweet chocolate, finely chopped

3 eggs

½ cup sugar

1¼ cups all-purpose flour

1¾ teaspoons baking powder

¾ teaspoon salt

1. Preheat oven to 300°F. Grease 8×4-inch loaf pan. Combine hazelnuts, figs, almonds, candied orange and lemon peels and chocolate in medium bowl; mix well.

2. Beat eggs and sugar in large bowl with electric mixer at high speed at least 5 minutes or until mixture is pale yellow and thick and fluffy. Gently fold nut mixture into egg mixture.

3. Combine flour, baking powder and salt in small bowl. Sift ½ of flour mixture over nut-egg mixture and gently fold in; repeat with remaining flour mixture.

4. Spread batter evenly into prepared pan. Bake 60 to 70 minutes until top is deep golden brown and firm to the touch. Cool in pan on wire rack 5 minutes. Remove loaf from pan; cool completely on wire rack at least 4 hours. Slice and serve.

Makes 12 to 16 servings

personal touch

CANDLES ADD DRAMA TO ANY PARTY SETTING. IF YOU LOVE THE IDEA OF CANDLELIGHT BUT HATE THE MESS CANDLES CAN MAKE, PLACE CANDLES IN THE FREEZER A DAY OR SO PRIOR TO YOUR PARTY. FREEZING CANDLES HELPS THEM TO DRIP LESS AND TO BURN MORE SLOWLY.

Fig and Hazelnut Cake

Strawberry Vanilla Cake

1 package DUNCAN
HINES® Moist
Deluxe® French
Vanilla Cake Mix

1 container DUNCAN
HINES® Creamy
Homestyle Vanilla
Buttercream
Frosting, divided

⅓ cup seedless
strawberry jam

Fresh strawberries, for
garnish (optional)

1. Preheat oven to 350°F. Grease and flour two 8- or 9-inch round pans.

2. Prepare, bake and cool cakes following package directions for basic recipe.

3. To assemble, place one cake layer on serving plate. Place ¼ cup Vanilla frosting in small resealable plastic bag. Snip off one corner. Pipe a bead of frosting on top of layer around outer edge. Fill remaining area with strawberry jam. Top with second cake layer. Spread remaining frosting on sides and top of cake. Decorate with fresh strawberries, if desired. *Makes 12 to 16 servings*

Tip: You may substitute Duncan Hines® Vanilla or Cream Cheese frosting for the Vanilla Buttercream frosting, if desired.

Carrot Cake with Easy Cream Cheese Frosting

1 package (2-layer size)
carrot cake mix

1 package (8 ounces)
PHILADELPHIA®
Cream Cheese,
softened

⅓ cup granulated *or*
powdered sugar

¼ cup cold milk

1 tub (8 ounces) COOL
WHIP® Whipped
Topping, thawed

PREPARE cake mix as directed on package for 13×9-inch pan. Cool completely.

BEAT cream cheese, sugar and milk in medium bowl with wire whisk until smooth. Gently stir in whipped topping. Spread over top of cake.

REFRIGERATE until ready to serve. Garnish as desired.

Makes 10 servings

Note: Substitute your favorite carrot cake recipe for carrot cake mix.

Prep Time: 20 minutes

Strawberry Vanilla Cake

Philadelphia® 3-Step® Crème Brûlée Cheesecake

2 packages (8 ounces each) PHILADELPHIA® Cream Cheese, softened

½ cup granulated sugar

1 teaspoon vanilla

2 eggs

1 egg yolk

1 ready-to-use graham cracker crust (6 ounces or 9-inch)

½ cup packed brown sugar

1 teaspoon water

1. MIX cream cheese, granulated sugar and vanilla at medium speed with electric mixer until well blended. Add eggs and egg yolk; mix until blended.

2. POUR into crust.

3. BAKE at 350°F, 40 minutes or until center is almost set. Cool. Refrigerate 3 hours or overnight. Just before serving, heat broiler. Mix brown sugar and water; spread over cheesecake. Place on cookie sheet. Broil 4 to 6 inches from heat 1 to 1½ minutes or until topping is bubbly.   *Makes 8 servings*

Prep Time: 10 minutes

Bake Time : 40 minutes

a helping hand

CRÈME BRÛLÉE LITERALLY MEANS "BURNT CREAM." IT DESCRIBES A CHILLED CUSTARD THAT IS TOPPED WITH BROWN SUGAR OR GRANULATED SUGAR AND THEN QUICKLY CARAMELIZED UNDER A BROILER TO CREATE A BRITTLE TOPPING. THE TOPPING PROVIDES A WONDERFUL TEXTURE CONTRAST TO THE CREAMY CUSTARD. IN THIS RECIPE, THE CHEESECAKE IS TOPPED WITH BROWN SUGAR AND BROILED TO RECREATE THE SAME FLAVOR AND TEXTURE CONTRAST.

Philadelphia® 3-Step® Crème Brûlée Cheesecake

Chocolate Raspberry Torte

1⅓ cups all-purpose flour

1 cup sugar, divided

1½ teaspoons baking powder

½ teaspoon salt

2 eggs, separated

1 cup (½ pint) cold whipping cream

½ teaspoon almond extract

CHOCOLATE FILLING & FROSTING (recipe follows)

½ cup sliced almonds

¼ cup seedless red raspberry preserves

Sweetened whipped topping (optional)

1. Heat oven to 350°F. Grease and flour two 8- or 9-inch round baking pans.

2. Stir together flour, ½ cup sugar, baking powder and salt; set aside. Beat egg whites in large bowl until foamy; gradually add ¼ cup sugar and beat until stiff peaks form. Beat 1 cup whipping cream in small bowl until stiff; fold into beaten egg whites.

3. Combine egg yolks, remaining ¼ cup sugar and almond extract in clean small bowl; beat on medium speed of mixer 3 minutes until thick and lemon colored. Gently fold into whipped cream mixture. Gradually fold in flour mixture into whipping cream mixture just until ingredients are blended (mixture will be thick). Divide batter evenly between prepared pans; smooth surface.

4. Bake 25 to 30 minutes or until cake springs back when touched lightly in center. Cool 5 minutes; remove from pans to wire racks. Cool completely.

5. Prepare CHOCOLATE FILLING & FROSTING. Split each cake layer in half horizontally. Place one layer on serving plate; spread with ⅔ cup CHOCLATE FILLING. Sprinkle with 1 tablespoon almonds; repeat with two more layers. Top with last layer; spread with raspberry preserves. Frost sides of cake with remaining filling. Garnish top edge with whipped cream, if desired. Sprinkle edge and center with remaining almonds; refrigerate until ready to serve. Cover; refrigerate leftover torte.   *Makes 16 servings*

CHOCOLATE FILLING & FROSTING: Stir together ⅔ cup sugar and ⅓ cup HERSHEY®S Cocoa in medium bowl. Add 1½ cups chilled whipping cream and 1½ teaspoons vanilla extract; beat until stiff. Makes about 3 cups.

Magnificent Pound Cake

CAKE

3 cups sugar

1 Butter Flavor*
    CRISCO® Stick or
    1 cup Butter Flavor*
    CRISCO® all-
    vegetable
    shortening plus
    additional for
    greasing

5 eggs

3⅓ cups all-purpose flour

½ teaspoon baking
    powder

½ teaspoon salt

1 cup milk

1 teaspoon coconut
    extract

1 teaspoon rum extract

GLAZE

½ cup sugar

¼ cup water

½ teaspoon pure almond
    extract

GARNISH (OPTIONAL)
Assorted fresh fruit

*Butter Flavor Crisco is
artificially flavored.*

1. Heat oven to 325°F. Grease 10-inch (12-cup) Bundt pan. Flour lightly.

2. For cake, combine 3 cups sugar and 1 cup shortening in large bowl. Beat at low speed of electric mixer until blended. Beat at medium speed until well blended. Add eggs, 1 at a time, beating 1 minute at low speed after each addition.

3. Combine flour, baking powder and salt in medium bowl. Add to creamed mixture alternately with milk, beginning and ending with flour mixture, beating at low speed after each addition until well blended. Add coconut extract and rum extract. Beat at medium speed 1 minute. Pour into pan.

4. Bake at 325°F for 1 hour 30 minutes to 1 hour 40 minutes or until toothpick inserted in center comes out clean. Cool 10 minutes before removing from pan. Place cake, fluted side up, on wire rack. Cool 20 minutes.

5. For glaze, combine ½ cup sugar, water and almond extract in small saucepan. Bring to a boil. Slide waxed paper under wire rack. Brush over warm cake, using all of glaze. Cool completely.

6. For optional garnish, place spoonful of assorted fresh fruit on each serving.

Makes one 10-inch Bundt Cake (12 to 16 servings)

Luscious Key Lime Cake

CAKE

1 package DUNCAN HINES® Moist Deluxe® Lemon Supreme Cake Mix

1 package (4-serving size) lemon instant pudding and pie filling mix

4 eggs

1 cup vegetable oil

¾ cup water

¼ cup Key lime juice (see Tip)

GLAZE

2 cups confectioners' sugar

⅓ cup Key lime juice

2 tablespoons water

2 tablespoons butter or margarine, melted

Additional confectioners' sugar

Lime slices, for garnish

Fresh strawberry slices, for garnish (optional)

1. Preheat oven to 350°F. Grease and flour 10-inch Bundt® or tube pan.

2. For cake, combine cake mix, pudding mix, eggs, oil, ¾ cup water and ¼ cup Key lime juice in large bowl. Beat at low speed with electric mixer until moistened. Beat at medium speed 2 minutes. Pour into pan. Bake at 350°F 50 to 60 minutes or until toothpick inserted in center comes out clean. Cool in pan 25 minutes. Remove cake from pan onto cooling rack. Return cake to pan. Poke holes in top of warm cake with toothpick or long-tined fork.

3. For glaze, combine 2 cups confectioners' sugar, ⅓ cup Key lime juice, 2 tablespoons water and melted butter in medium bowl. Pour slowly over top of warm cake. Cool completely. Invert onto serving plate. Dust with additional confectioners' sugar. Garnish with lime slices and strawberry slices, if desired.

Makes 12 to 16 servings

Tip: Fresh or bottled lime juice may be substituted for the Key lime juice.

Luscious Key Lime Cake

Heavenly Cheesecake

½ cup graham cracker crumbs

4 packages (8 ounces each) PHILADELPHIA BRAND® Neufchâtel Cheese, ⅓ Less Fat Than Cream Cheese

1 cup sugar

¼ teaspoon almond extract or 1 teaspoon vanilla

2 eggs

3 egg whites

• HEAT oven to 325°F.

• GREASE bottom of 9-inch springform pan. Sprinkle with crumbs.

• BEAT Neufchâtel cheese, sugar and extract at medium speed with electric mixer until well blended. Add eggs and egg whites, 1 at a time, mixing at low speed after each addition, just until blended. Pour into pan.

• BAKE 45 to 50 minutes or until center is almost set. Run knife or metal spatula around rim of pan to loosen cake; cool before removing rim of pan. Refrigerate 4 hours or overnight.

• GARNISH with raspberries, strawberries or blueberries and mint leaves. *Makes 12 servings*

Prep Time: 15 minutes

Bake Time: 50 minutes

Bourbon Pecan Pie

Pastry for a single-crust 9-inch pie

¼ cup butter or margarine, softened

½ cup sugar

3 eggs

1½ cups light or dark corn syrup

2 tablespoons bourbon

1 teaspoon vanilla extract

1 cup pecan halves

Preheat oven to 350°F. Roll out pastry and line 9-inch pie pan; flute edge. Beat butter in large bowl of electric mixer on medium speed until creamy. Add sugar; beat until fluffy. Add eggs, one at a time, beating well after each addition. Add corn syrup, bourbon and vanilla; beat until well blended. Pour filling into pastry shell. Arrange pecan halves on top. Bake on lowest oven rack 50 to 55 minutes or until knife inserted slightly off center comes out clean (filling will be puffy). Place on rack and cool. Serve at room temperature or refrigerate up to 24 hours.

Makes 6 to 8 servings

Heavenly Cheesecake

Cider Apple Pie in Cheddar Crust

CRUST

2 cups sifted all-purpose flour

1 cup shredded Cheddar cheese

½ teaspoon salt

⅔ CRISCO® Stick or ⅔ cup CRISCO® all-vegetable shortening

5 to 6 tablespoons ice water

FILLING

6 cups sliced, peeled apples (about 2 pounds or 6 medium)

1 cup apple cider

⅔ cup sugar

2 tablespoons cornstarch

2 tablespoons water

½ teaspoon cinnamon

1 tablespoon butter or margarine

GLAZE

1 egg yolk

1 tablespoon water

1. Heat oven to 400°F.

2. For crust, place flour, cheese and salt in food processor bowl. Add shortening. Process 15 seconds. Sprinkle water through food chute, 1 tablespoon at a time, until dough just forms (process time not to exceed 20 seconds). Shape into ball. Divide dough in half. Press between hands to form two 5- to 6-inch "pancakes." Roll and press bottom crust into 9-inch pie plate.

3. For filling, combine apples, apple cider and sugar in large saucepan. Cook and stir on medium-high heat until mixture comes to a boil. Reduce heat to low. Simmer 5 minutes. Combine cornstarch, water and cinnamon. Stir into apples. Cook and stir until mixture comes to a boil. Remove from heat. Stir in butter. Spoon into unbaked pie crust. Moisten pastry edge with water.

4. Roll top crust same as bottom. Lift onto filled pie. Trim ½ inch beyond edge of pie plate. Fold top edge under bottom crust. Flute. Cut slits or design in top crust to allow steam to escape.

5. For glaze, beat egg yolk with fork. Stir in water. Brush over top.

6. Bake at 400°F for 35 to 40 minutes or until filling in center is bubbly and crust is golden brown. Cover edge with foil, if necessary, to prevent overbrowning. *Do not overbake.* Cool to room temperature before serving.   *Makes 1 (9-inch) pie*

Note: Golden Delicious, Granny Smith and Jonathan apples are all suitable for pie baking.

Cider Apple Pie in Cheddar Crust

Fresh Fruit Tart

1⅔ cups all-purpose flour

⅓ cup sugar

¼ teaspoon salt

½ cup butter or margarine, softened and cut into pieces

1 egg yolk

2 to 3 tablespoons milk

1 package (8 ounces) regular or reduced-calorie cream cheese, softened

⅓ cup strawberry jam

2 to 3 cups mixed assorted fresh fruit, such as sliced bananas, sliced kiwi, blueberries, sliced peaches, sliced plums, raspberries and halved strawberries

¼ cup apple jelly, melted

¼ cup toasted sliced unblanched almonds (optional)

1. Combine flour, sugar and salt in food processor or blender; process until just combined. Add butter. Process using on/off pulsing action until mixture resembles coarse crumbs. Add egg yolk and 2 tablespoons milk; process until dough leaves side of bowl. Add additional milk by teaspoons, if necessary. Shape dough into a disc. Wrap in plastic wrap and refrigerate 30 minutes or until firm.

2. Preheat oven to 350°F. Roll dough out on lightly floured surface to ¼-inch thickness. Cut 12-inch circle; transfer to 10-inch tart pan with removable bottom. Press lightly onto bottom and up side of pan; trim edges even with edge of pan. Bake 16 to 18 minutes or until light golden brown. Transfer to wire rack; cool completely.

3. Combine cream cheese and jam in small bowl; mix well. Spread evenly over cooled crust. Arrange fruit decoratively over cream cheese layer. Brush fruit with apple jelly. Sprinkle with almonds, if desired. Serve immediately or refrigerate up to 2 hours before serving.

Makes 8 servings

Fresh Fruit Tart

Cherry Crisp

1 (21-ounce) can cherry
   pie filling or
   topping

½ teaspoon almond
   extract

½ cup all-purpose flour

½ cup firmly packed
   brown sugar

1 teaspoon ground
   cinnamon

3 tablespoons butter or
   margarine, softened

½ cup chopped walnuts

¼ cup flaked coconut

   Ice cream or whipped
   cream

Pour cherry pie filling into ungreased 8-inch square baking pan. Stir in almond extract.

Combine flour, brown sugar and cinnamon in medium mixing bowl; mix well. Add butter; stir with fork until mixture is crumbly. Stir in walnuts and coconut. Sprinkle mixture over cherry pie filling.

Bake in preheated 350°F oven 25 minutes or until golden brown on top and filling is bubbly. Serve warm or at room temperature. If desired, top with ice cream or whipped cream.

Makes 6 servings

Note: This recipe can be doubled. Bake in two 8-inch square baking pans or one 13×9×2-inch pan.

Favorite recipe from Cherry Marketing Institute, Inc.

personal touch

TURN THIS DELICIOUS DESSERT INTO THE PERFECT HOSTESS GIFT. COMBINE THE FLOUR, SUGAR AND CINNAMON IN A GLASS JAR WITH A TIGHT FITTING LID. PLACE THE WALNUTS AND COCONUT IN A SEPARATE CONTAINER. PLACE BOTH CONTAINERS, THE CAN OF CHERRY PIE FILLING AND THE RECIPE FOR THIS CHERRY CRISP IN A DECORATIVE BASKET. TIE IT ALL UP WITH A BEAUTIFUL KITCHEN TOWEL AND YOUR GIFT IS READY TO GO.

Cherry Crisp

Amaretto Cheesecake Tart

CRUST

¾ cup amaretti cookie crumbs

¾ cup zwieback crumbs

1 tablespoon sugar

¼ cup Prune Purée (recipe follows) or prepared prune butter

FILLING

1 carton (16 ounces) nonfat cottage cheese

4 ounces fat-free cream cheese, softened

2 eggs

2 tablespoons almond-flavored liqueur

TOPPING & GLAZE

2 oranges, peeled and sliced into rounds

1 kiwifruit, peeled and sliced into rounds

2 tablespoons apple jelly, melted

Fresh raspberries, orange peel and mint leaves for garnish

Preheat oven to 325°F. To prepare crust, in medium bowl, combine crumbs and sugar. Cut in Prune Purée with pastry blender until mixture resembles coarse crumbs. Press onto bottom and side of 9-inch tart pan with removable bottom. To prepare filling, process cottage cheese and cream cheese in food processor 3 to 5 minutes or until smooth. Add eggs and liqueur; process until blended. Pour into prepared crust. Bake in center of oven 30 minutes or until filling is set. Cool on wire rack; refrigerate until completely chilled. Arrange fruit on top of filling. Brush fruit with jelly. Garnish with raspberries, orange peel and mint. Cut into wedges. *Makes 10 servings*

Prune Purée: Combine 1⅓ cups (8 ounces) pitted prunes and 6 tablespoons hot water in container of food processor or blender. Pulse on and off until prunes are finely chopped and smooth. Store leftovers in a covered container in the refrigerator for up to two months. Makes 1 cup.

Favorite recipe from California Prune Board

Amaretto Cheesecake Tart

Chocolate Hazelnut Pie

Chocolate Hazelnut Crust (recipe follows)

1 envelope unflavored gelatin

¼ cup cold water

2 cups whipping cream, divided

1½ cups semisweet chocolate chips

½ cup liquid egg substitute

3 tablespoons hazelnut-flavored liqueur

1 teaspoon vanilla

24 caramels, unwrapped

1. Prepare Chocolate Hazelnut Crust; set aside.

2. Sprinkle gelatin over water in small saucepan. Let stand without stirring 3 minutes for gelatin to soften. Heat over low heat, stirring constantly, until gelatin is completely dissolved, about 5 minutes.

3. Stir 1 cup whipping cream into gelatin mixture. Heat just to a boil; remove from heat. Add chocolate chips. Stir until chocolate is melted.

4. Add ½ cup whipping cream, egg substitute, liqueur and vanilla; beat well. Pour into large bowl; refrigerate about 15 minutes or until thickened.

5. Combine caramels and remaining ½ cup whipping cream in small saucepan. Simmer over low heat, stirring occasionally, until completely melted and smooth.

6. Pour caramel mixture into prepared crust; let stand about 10 minutes.

7. Beat thickened gelatin mixture with electric mixer at medium speed until smooth. Pour over caramel layer; refrigerate 3 hours or until firm. Garnish, if desired. *Makes 6 to 8 servings*

Chocolate Hazelnut Crust

30 chocolate cookie wafers

¾ cup hazelnuts, toasted

½ cup melted butter or margarine

1. Preheat oven to 350°F.

2. Combine cookies and hazelnuts in food processor or blender; process with on/off pulses until finely crushed.

3. Combine cookie mixture and butter in medium bowl. Press firmly onto bottom and up side of 9-inch pie plate, forming high rim.

4. Bake 10 minutes; cool on wire rack.

Strawberry Margarita Pie

1 ¼ **cups crushed pretzels**

¼ **cup sugar**

10 **tablespoons butter** *or* **margarine, melted**

1 **can (14 ounces) sweetened condensed milk**

2 **cups strawberries, crushed or puréed**

½ **cup lime juice**

1 **tub (8 ounces) COOL WHIP® Whipped Topping, thawed**

MIX pretzels, sugar and butter in 9-inch pie plate. Press mixture onto bottom and up side of pie plate. Refrigerate until ready to fill.

MIX condensed milk, strawberries and lime juice in large bowl until well blended. Gently stir in whipped topping. Pour into prepared crust.

FREEZE 6 hours or overnight. Let stand at room temperature 15 minutes or until pie can be cut easily. Garnish with additional whipped topping, strawberries and lime peel, if desired.

Makes 8 servings

Helpful Hint: Dip pie plate into warm water, just to rim, for 30 seconds for easy serving.

Note: Two prepared graham cracker crumb crusts (6 ounces *or* 9 inches each) can be substituted for the homemade crust. Divide filling equally between the 2 pie crusts.

Lime Margarita Pie: Omit strawberries and lime juice; add one 12-ounce can lime juice concentrate; proceed as above.

Prep Time: 10 minutes

personal touch

FLOWERS ABOUND! SKIP THE TRADITIONAL BOUQUET OF FLOWERS IN THE CENTER OF THE TABLE AND GIVE EACH GUEST HIS OR HER OWN UNIQUE BOUQUET. MAKE MINI-ARRANGEMENTS IN DIFFERENT SHAPED JUICE GLASSES AND PLACE THEM AT EACH PERSON'S PLACE SETTING.

Pear Cherry Strudel

4 cups cored pared sliced Northwest winter pears

1 tablespoon lemon juice

½ cup fine vanilla wafer crumbs

½ cup dried cherries

¼ cup sugar

1 ½ teaspoons grated lemon peel

½ teaspoon ground cinnamon

8 sheets fillo dough

⅓ cup butter, melted

Powdered sugar

Unsweetened whipped cream or vanilla ice cream

Preheat oven to 400°F. Toss pears with lemon juice in large bowl. Combine crumbs, cherries, sugar, lemon peel and cinnamon in small bowl; mix well. Sprinkle over pears; stir gently to mix. Unroll sheets of fillo dough; cover with waxed paper and dampened towel. Keep dough under towel at all times. Working on a towel, layer fillo dough, brushing each sheet with butter. Place pear mixture down long edge of fillo in 3-inch strip. Using towel under dough, gently lift and roll fillo, jelly roll fashion. Carefully place on baking sheet. Brush with butter. Bake 25 to 30 minutes or until golden brown. Cool slightly; dust with powdered sugar. Serve warm or cool. *Makes 10 to 12 servings*

Favorite recipe from Oregon-Washington-California Pear Bureau

personal touch

TIGHT ON SPACE? IF YOU ARE AFRAID YOUR TABLE IS TOO SMALL TO ACCOMMODATE ALL YOUR GUESTS, AVOID USING PLACE MATS. USE A TABLE CLOTH OR NOTHING AT ALL. THIS WILL HELP YOU TO BE ABLE TO PUT PLACE SETTINGS CLOSER TOGETHER. ALSO, TRY TO AVOID USING OVERSIZED CHAIRS AS THIS WILL TAKE UP VALUABLE SEATING SPACE.

Pear Cherry Strudel

Cappucino Bon Bons

1 package DUNCAN HINES® Chocolate Lovers Chewy Fudge Brownie Mix, Family Size

⅓ cup water

⅓ cup canola oil

2 eggs

1½ tablespoons instant coffee

1 teaspoon ground cinnamon

Whipped topping

Cinnamon

1. Preheat oven to 350°F. Place 2-inch foil cupcake liners on cookie sheet.

2. Combine brownie mix, water, oil, eggs, instant coffee and cinnamon. Stir with spoon until well blended, about 50 strokes. Fill each cupcake liner with 1 measuring tablespoon batter. Bake 12 to 15 minutes or until wooden toothpick inserted in center comes out clean. Cool completely. Garnish with whipped topping and a dash of cinnamon. Refrigerate until ready to serve.

Makes about 40 bon bons

Tip: To make larger Bon Bons, use twelve 2½-inch foil cupcake liners and fill with ¼ cup batter. Bake 28 to 30 minutes.

Chocolate-Dipped Strawberry Parfaits

1 package (8 squares) BAKER'S® Semi-Sweet Chocolate

2 teaspoons butter or shortening

3 pints small strawberries, hulled

1 tub (8 ounces) COOL WHIP® Whipped Topping, thawed

Fresh mint leaves

MICROWAVE chocolate and butter in small microwavable bowl on HIGH 1½ to 2 minutes or until chocolate is almost melted, stirring halfway through heating time. Stir until chocolate is completely melted.

DIP strawberries into chocolate to coat at least ½ of the berry. Place on wax paper; let stand until chocolate is firm.

LAYER about 6 chocolate-dipped strawberries and ⅓ cup whipped topping in each of 8 dessert glasses just before serving. Garnish with mint leaves.

Makes 8 servings

Cappucino Bon Bons

Candied Citrus Peel

6 large, thick-skinned oranges

5½ cups water

5 cups sugar, divided

Remove peel from white part of oranges in long strips with sharp paring knife. Reserve fruit for another use. Discard all pithy fruit membranes from peel. Cut peel into 2×½-inch strips. (There will be some oddly shaped pieces.) Place sheet of waxed paper under wire rack. Bring 4 cups water to a boil in heavy 3-quart saucepan over high heat. Add peel; return to a boil. Reduce heat to low. Cover; cook 20 minutes. Drain. Repeat process 2 times.

Bring 4½ cups sugar and 1½ cups water to a boil in same saucepan over medium heat, stirring occasionally. Reduce heat to low. Carefully clip candy thermometer to side of pan (do not let bulb touch bottom of pan). Cook over low heat about 20 minutes or until thermometer registers 230°F, without stirring. Add drained peel. Cook over low heat about 20 minutes more or until thermometer registers 240°F (soft-ball stage), stirring occasionally. Remove from heat. Remove strips with slotted spoon to wire rack over waxed paper. Discard syrup or save for another use. Cool strips until syrup has dripped off.

Put remaining ½ cup sugar on another sheet of waxed paper. Roll strips, one at a time, in sugar. Set strips on wire rack about 1 hour or until dry. Store in airtight container. Keep in a cool place up to 2 weeks. If strips become slightly sticky, roll again in additional sugar.   *Makes about 90 strips*

Variation: Melt ½ cup semisweet chocolate chips and 1 tablespoon butter in small saucepan over low heat, stirring until smooth. Dip one end of each strip in melted chocolate; set on wire rack over waxed paper to dry. Let chocolate set completely before storing in airtight container.

personal touch

LOOKING FOR SOMETHING DIFFERENT TO TAKE TO YOUR HOLIDAY GATHERING? DECORATE A METAL TIN WITH RUBBER STAMPS FOR A FUN CRAFTY LOOK. FILL IT WITH CANDIED CITRUS PEEL AND PACKETS OF GOURMET COFFEE.

Candied Citrus Peel

Classic Peanut Brittle

**MAZOLA NO STICK®
Cooking Spray**

**1 cup KARO® Light or
Dark Corn Syrup**

1 cup sugar

¼ cup water

**2 tablespoons MAZOLA®
Margarine or butter**

1½ cups peanuts

1 teaspoon baking soda

1. Spray large cookie sheet and metal spatula with cooking spray; set aside.

2. In heavy 3-quart saucepan combine corn syrup, sugar, water and margarine. Stirring constantly, cook over medium heat until sugar dissolves and mixture comes to boil.

3. Without stirring, cook until temperature reaches 280°F on candy thermometer or small amount of mixture dropped into very cold water separates into threads which are hard but not brittle.

4. Gradually stir in peanuts. Stirring frequently, continue cooking until temperature reaches 300°F or small amount of mixture dropped into very cold water separates into threads which are hard and brittle. Remove from heat; stir in baking soda.

5. Immediately pour mixture onto cookie sheet. With metal spatula, spread mixture evenly to edges. Cool. Break into pieces.

Makes about 1½ pounds

Prep Time: **60 minutes, plus cooling**

Mango Coconut Tropical Freeze

**1 jar (26 ounces)
refrigerated mango
slices, drained (or
the flesh of 3 ripe
mangoes, peeled
and cut to equal
about 3⅓ cups)**

**½ cup canned coconut
cream**

1 tablespoon lime juice

**⅓ cup toasted chopped
pecans**

1. Place mango, coconut cream and lime juice in food processor; process 1 to 2 minutes or until smooth.

2. Spoon into small dessert cups or custard cups. Top with pecans. Place cups on pie plate; cover tightly. Freeze 8 hours or overnight. Remove from freezer and allow to thaw slightly before serving. Serve immediately.

Makes 4 servings

Mango Coconut Tropical Freeze

Holiday Chocolate Berry Trifle

3 cups cold milk

2 packages (4-serving size each) JELL-O® Chocolate Flavor Instant Pudding & Pie Filling

1 tub (12 ounces) COOL WHIP® Whipped Topping, thawed

1 baked 9-inch square brownie layer, cut into 1-inch cubes

1 pint raspberries

POUR cold milk into large bowl. Add pudding mixes. Beat with wire whisk 2 minutes. Gently stir in 2 cups whipped topping.

PLACE half of the brownie cubes in 2-quart serving bowl. Top with half of the pudding mixture, half of the raspberries and 2 cups whipped topping. Repeat layers. Top with remaining whipped topping.

REFRIGERATE 1 hour or until ready to serve.

Makes 12 servings

Prep Time: 15 minutes

Brownie Baked Alaskas

2 purchased brownies (2½ inches square)

2 scoops fudge swirl ice cream (or favorite flavor)

⅓ cup semisweet chocolate chips

2 tablespoons light corn syrup or milk

2 egg whites

¼ cup sugar

1. Preheat oven to 500°F. Place brownies on small cookie sheet; top each with scoop of ice cream and place in freezer.

2. Melt chocolate chips in small saucepan over low heat. Stir in corn syrup; set aside and keep warm.

3. Beat egg whites to soft peaks in small bowl. Gradually beat in sugar; continue beating until stiff peaks form. Spread over ice cream and brownies with small spatula (ice cream and brownies should be completely covered with egg white mixture).

4. Bake 2 to 3 minutes or until meringue is golden. Spread chocolate sauce on serving plates; place baked Alaskas over sauce.

Makes 2 servings

Brownie Baked Alaskas

Simple Peach Sorbet

1 can (15¼ ounces) DEL MONTE® Peaches in Heavy Syrup

1 teaspoon vanilla extract

1. Place unopened can of fruit in freezer; freeze until solid, approximately 24 hours. (Can may bulge slightly.) Submerge unopened frozen can in very hot tap water for 1 minute. Open can and pour any thawed syrup into food processor bowl.* Remove frozen fruit from can.

2. Cut fruit into 8 chunks. Place frozen fruit chunks in food processor; add vanilla. Process until smooth, scraping blade as needed. Serve immediately or spoon into freezer container and freeze until desired firmness.   *Makes 3 servings*

Not recommended for blenders or mini food processors.

Piña Colada Sorbet: Follow above directions using 1 can DEL MONTE® Pineapple in Heavy Syrup, 2½ tablespoons well-chilled coconut milk, and if desired, ½ tablespoon rum or ½ teaspoon rum extract.

Pear-Ginger Sorbet: Follow above directions using 1 can DEL MONTE® Pears in Heavy Syrup and ½ teaspoon minced ginger root.

Note: To double recipe, process in two separate batches.

Prep Time: 8 minutes

a helping hand

KEEP IT ICY! PLACE YOUR DESSERT DISHES AND SPOONS IN THE FREEZER UNTIL FROSTED. WHEN READY TO SERVE THE SORBET, SCOOP IT INTO THE FROSTED DISHES FOR A REFRESHING TREAT EVERYONE WILL ENJOY.

Old-Fashioned Creamy Fudge

2 cups sugar

¾ cup milk

2½ bars (1 ounce each)
   HERSHEY'S
   Unsweetened
   Baking Chocolate,
   broken into pieces

2 tablespoons light corn
   syrup

¼ teaspoon salt

2 tablespoons butter

1 teaspoon vanilla
   extract

1. Line 8-inch square pan with foil, extending foil over edges of pan. Lightly butter foil.

2. Stir together sugar, milk, baking chocolate, corn syrup and salt in heavy 2-quart saucepan. Cook over medium heat, stirring constantly, until mixture comes to full rolling boil. Cook, stirring occasionally, until mixture reaches 234°F on candy thermometer or until small amount of mixture dropped into very cold water forms a soft ball, which flattens when removed from water. (Bulb of candy thermometer should not rest on bottom of saucepan.)

3. Remove from heat. Add butter and vanilla. DO NOT STIR. Cool at room temperature to 110°F (lukewarm). Beat with wooden spoon until fudge thickens and just begins to lose some of its gloss. Quickly spread into prepared pan. Cool completely. Cut into squares. Store in tightly covered container at room temperature.

Makes about 3 dozen pieces or 1½ pounds

Note: For best results, do not double this recipe.

Prep Time: 20 minutes

Cook Time: 25 minutes

Cool Time: 2½ hours

Bananas Flambé

1 large banana

4 teaspoons honey

4 teaspoons chopped walnuts

4 teaspoons brandy (optional)

Halve unpeeled banana lengthwise; place in small flameproof dish. Drizzle cut surface of each half with 2 teaspoons honey and sprinkle with walnuts. On top rack of preheated oven broiler, broil banana about 5 minutes or until heated but not burnt. Remove from broiler. If desired, pour brandy over top and flame.

Makes 2 servings

Tip: Orange blossom honey is particularly good in this dessert.

Tangy Pineapple Fondue

1 (8-ounce) can crushed pineapple in its own juice, undrained

1 cup apple juice

¼ cup A.1.® Steak Sauce

¼ cup firmly packed light brown sugar

1 tablespoon cornstarch

1 medium pineapple, cut into chunks

1 (12-ounce) package prepared pound cake, cut into 1-inch cubes

1 pint strawberries, halved

1 large Granny Smith apple, cored and cut into chunks

In small saucepan, combine crushed pineapple, apple juice, steak sauce, brown sugar and cornstarch until blended. Over medium heat, cook and stir pineapple mixture until boiling; reduce heat. Simmer 1 minute; keep warm.

Alternately thread pineapple chunks and cake cubes onto 16 (10-inch) metal skewers. Over medium heat, grill kabobs until lightly toasted, about 3 to 5 minutes, turning occasionally. Remove pineapple chunks and cake cubes from skewers; arrange on large platter with remaining fruit. Serve with warm sauce for dipping.

Makes 16 servings

acknowledgments

The publishers would like to thank the companies and organizations listed below for the use of their recipes and photographs in this publication.

A.1.® Steak Sauce

Almond Board of California

Bestfoods

Birds Eye®

Bob Evans®

Butterball® Turkey Company

California Prune Board

California Tree Fruit Agreement

Campbell Soup Company

Cherry Marketing Institute

ConAgra Grocery Products Company

Del Monte Corporation

Dole Food Company, Inc.

Duncan Hines® and Moist Deluxe® are registered trademarks of Aurora Foods Inc.

Egg Beaters®

Pear Bureau Northwest

Fleischmann's® Original Spread

Florida Department of Agriculture and Consumer Services, Bureau of Seafood and Aquaculture

Grey Poupon® Mustard

Hebrew National®

Hershey Foods Corporation

Hillshire Farm®

The HV Company

Kikkoman International Inc.

Kraft Foods, Inc.

Land O' Lakes, Inc.

Lawry's® Foods, Inc.

Lipton®

M&M/MARS

McIlhenny Company (TABASCO® brand Pepper Sauce)

National Cattlemen's Beef Association

National Honey Board

Newman's Own, Inc.®

North Dakota Beef Commission

OREO® Cookies

The Procter & Gamble Company

The Quaker® Oatmeal Kitchens

Reckitt & Colman Inc.

The J.M. Smucker Company

Sonoma® Dried Tomatoes

Sun•Maid® Growers of California

Uncle Ben's Inc.

USA Rice Federation

Walnut Marketing Board

Washington Apple Commission

Wisconsin Milk Marketing Board

index